HUSBANDS, LOVE YOUR WIVES...

A Collection of Devotions for Husbands and Wives

Ephesians 5:25-31

Bobby & Pam Sanders

A Husbands, Love Your Wives Publication

Husbands, Love Your Wives Publications
P. O. Box 2142
Harker Heights, TX 76548-2142
Phone: (254) 699-3785
LOVEYOURWIVES@AOL.COM

ISBN 1-59196-057-6

Printed in the U. S. A. by Instantpublisher.com.

SPECIAL THANKS

Above all, we give all Praise, all Glory, all Honor, and all appreciation to God Almighty, our Heavenly Father; and to His Son, our Lord and Savior, Jesus Christ, and to Holy Spirit (the Third Person of the Trinity). We thank God for His precious gift of salvation through His Son Jesus Christ. There is none like Him. We thank Him for giving us patients and an ear to hear what the Spirit of the Lord is saying.

We thank God for the readers of our weekly e-mail devotions. Thanks for your encouragement. Thank you for allowing us to share with you what God has given us.

We thank God for Mrs. Latorial Faison. God has used her in a special way to make this publication possible. She is a Christian and founder of "Poetically Speaking Publications." http://www.poeticallyspeaking.net. We strongly recommend the use of her publishing company.

We thank God for our parents (deceased and alive) for their love, care and concern.

To My Noble Wife, Pam:

I thank God for you. You are a special woman of God, sent by God, and anointed by God. Besides God, I am thankful that you are everything I need. I need not look any further. You are a part of me. You make me complete. You are my honey, my sweetheart, my Queen, my lover, and most importantly my best friend. I love you!

Bobby

This copy of

HUSBANDS, LOVE YOUR WIVES...

A Collection of Devotions for Husbands and Wives

is presented to

____

____

by

____

on

____

Husbands, Love Your Wives Publications

CONTENTS

DEVOTIONS

INTRODUCTION

The weekly e-mail devotion **"Husbands, Love Your Wives...,"** for men and women (husbands and wives) has inspired this book.

The best, most secure marriages are constantly under attack. It has been placed on our hearts to encourage husbands and wives and offer God's perspective about marriage. This is not suggesting that your marriage is in trouble, it is just a tool that you can use to enrich your marriage. Each article includes practical ways to apply the thought and a way to be a blessing to your wife. After all, marriage is "until death do you part." The articles are brief and applicable to the challenges marriages face today. So take an article and focus on it for a week by reading it at least once each day. Use them as a means to rejuvenate your marriage and keep it rejuvenated.

God tells us that marriage should be honored among all. Marriage is important to God and anything that's important to God is important to us. Marriage takes on new meaning when viewed as God views it. Inside, we offer you God's perspective.

We are confident that this book will encourage you in your marriage. But like medicine – if you don't take it as prescribed, it won't do you any good just sitting on the counter. We encourage you to get the Word of God down in your spirit.

We also want you to know that this book is to enhance marriages. It was not inspired to take anything away from you, your home, your church, or your marriage. We welcome your prayers, and you are free to recommend this book to others.

If you are not getting the weekly e-mail devotions contact us by e-mail or write us to subscribe (see page 132). Devotions are available through regular mail.

Although the title of this book says "Husbands," we strongly encourage wives to read it also. It will bless you. We also have a weekly e-mail devotion, just for the wives at: anoblewife@aol.com.

We value your comments, so if you find this book encouraging, exciting, or helpful, please tell someone and let us know by writing or e-mailing us (see page 132). Thank you in advance, and may God continue to richly bless you and your family.

OUR VISION

Our vision is to reach, encourage, and minister to millions of husbands and wives through Godly-inspired e-mail devotions, mailings, publications, and an Internet web site.
Bottom line:
"We want to positively impact marriages."

WE BELIEVE:

that Jesus is the Son of God
that Jesus was born of the Virgin Mary
that Jesus is the same yesterday, today, and forever
that Jesus' death on the Cross paid the penalty for our sins
that Jesus' shed blood will never lose its power
that Jesus was buried and was resurrected three day later
that Jesus is now at the right hand of the Father
that the Holy Ghost is with us today fulfilling God's divine purposes
that God ordained marriages from the beginning
that marriage is "until death do you part"
that God allowed divorce because of the hardness of man's heart
that marriage is sacred and honorable
that marriage is between one man and one woman
that what God has joined together let not man separate
that Jesus is the Way, the Truth, and the Life and that no one comes to the Father except by Him.

We believe that the entire Holy Bible is the inspired Word of God.

ABOUT THE AUTHORS

Bobby and Pam were both born and raised in North Carolina. Bobby joined the United States Army in May 1977 as a Personnel Specialist. Pam and Bobby, who were neighborhood sweethearts, married in July 1978. Their numerous assignments in the military took them to Fort Bragg, NC; San Diego, CA; Ludwigsburg, Germany; Fort Gordon, GA; Fort Monmouth, NJ; Schofield Barracks, HI; Fort Drum, NY; Fort Shafter, HI; Fort Bliss, TX, and Fort Hood, TX. After years of travel they currently reside in the Fort Hood/Killeen, TX area.

They became born-again Christians and members of The City of Refuge Christian Church (CORCC) while in Hawaii (November 1991). They have two daughters, one son, and five granddaughters.

They also have a weekly e-mail devotion ministry for the wives. The ministry is called:

"A Wife of Noble Character,"
anoblewife@aol.com.

Bobby is a licensed minister and Pam is a licensed deaconess (since 1996) through The City of Refuge Christian Church of Northern New York in Great Bend, New York.

They are currently members of The People's Choice Worship Center, Killeen, Texas.

IMPACT OF CHRISTIAN LEADERS

We thank God for the impact of Christian Leaders in our lives. Over the years, there have been numerous Christian leaders who have made significant spiritual contributions in our lives. They include (but are not limited to):

Bishop (Doctor) Wayne E. Anderson, Pastor of the City of Refuge Christian Church (CORCC), Waipahu, Hawaii. Dr. Anderson was our very first pastor from November 1991 to June 1992. God used him to lay a solid spiritual foundation in our lives through uncompromising teaching and preaching.

Elder John W. Jordan, Pastor, CORCC of Northern New York, Great Bend, New York. Elder Jordan was our pastor from July 1992 to July 1997 (not just a pastor, but a great friend). God used him to build on the foundation and to encourage spiritual growth.

Elder Jeff Carter, Pastor, in Buffalo, New York and his wife Evangelist Debbie are true friends and caring servants of God who have truly been role models.

Elder Charles Givens, Pastor, in Augusta, Georgia, is a preacher that God has used over the years to take us to higher levels in Christ.

Deacon Willie and Evangelist Stephanie Bond, of Minneapolis, Minnesota always bring a fresh, new revelation of the Word to us.

Deacon Albert and Pastor Ann Newell, of Fayetteville, NC are friends who always believe the best in everyone.

Brother Glenn and Sister Louisa Butler, longtime members of the CORCC in Hawaii played a major part in our coming to know Jesus Christ as our personal Savior and Lord. The Butlers continue to show love in a supernatural way.

Brother John Baronne, President, Full Gospel Businessmen's Fellowship International, Watertown, New York Chapter and his wife Sister Shirley; he should have been known as "Barnabas" for his manifested comfort to the brotherhood of believers.

Bishop T.D. Jakes, Pastor, The Potter's House, Dallas, Texas. Although he may not know it, his teachings and preaching motivated us to start the weekly e-mail devotion, which later led to this book.

Pastors Jackie and Dale Clay of Agape Fellowship, El Paso, Texas made this ministry available world wide via the Internet.

Bishop George Williams and Mother Clemmie Williams of The People's Choice Worship Center, Killeen, Texas is our Pastor and First Lady. They are a man and woman of God who preach, teach, and live the Godly marriage.

Scriptural Foundation for "Husbands, Love your Wives..."

Ephesians 5:25-33

New International Version (NIV)

Husbands, love your wives, just as Christ loved the church and gave himself up for her to make her holy, cleansing her by the washing with water through the word, and to present her to himself as a radiant church, without stain or wrinkle or any other blemish, but holy and blameless. In this same way, husbands ought to love their wives as their own bodies. He who loves his wife loves himself. After all, no one ever hated his own body, but he feeds and cares for it, just as Christ does the church - for we are members of his body. "For this reason a man will leave his father and mother and be united to his wife, and the Two will become one flesh." This is a profound mystery - but I am talking about Christ and the church. However, each one of you also must love his wife as he loves himself, and the wife must respect her husband.

The Living Bible (TLB)

And you husbands, show the same kind of love to your wives as Christ showed to the Church when he died for her, to make her holy and clean, washed by baptism and God's Word; so that he could give her to himself as a glorious Church without a single spot or wrinkle or any other blemish, being holy and without a single fault. That is how husbands should treat their wives, loving them as parts of themselves. For since a man and his wife are now one, a man is really doing himself a favor and loving himself when he loves his wife! No one hates his own body but lovingly cares for it, just as Christ cares for his body the Church, of which we are parts. (That the husband and wife are one body is proved by the Scripture which says, "A man must leave his father and mother when he marries, so that he can be perfectly joined to his wife, and the two shall be one.") I know this is hard to understand, but it is an illustration of the way we are parts of the body of Christ. So again I say, a man must love his wife as a part of himself; and the wife must see to it that she deeply respects her husband – obeying, praising and honoring him.

The Amplified Bible (AMP)

Husbands, love your wives, as Christ loved the church and gave himself up for her, so that He might sanctify her, having cleansed her by the washing of water with the Word, that He might present the church to Himself in glorious splendor, without spot or wrinkle or any such things [that she might be holy and faultless]. Even so husbands should love their wives as [being in a sense] their own bodies. He who loves his own wife loves himself. For no man ever hated his own flesh, but nourishes *and* carefully protects and cherishes it, as Christ does the church. Because we are members (parts) of His body. For this reason a man shall leave his father and his mother and shall be joined to his wife, and the two shall become one flesh. This mystery is very great, but I speak concerning [the relation of] Christ and the church. However, let each man of you [without exception] love his wife as [being in a sense] his very own self; and let the wife see that she respects *and* reverences her husband [that she notices him, regards him, honors him, prefers him, venerates, and esteems him; and that she defers to him, praises him, and loves and admires him exceedingly].

The King James Version (KJV)

Husbands, love your wives, even as Christ also loved the church, and gave himself for it; that he might sanctify and cleanse it with the washing of water by the word, that he might present it to himself a glorious church, not having spot, or wrinkle, or any such thing; but that it should be holy and without blemish. So ought men to love their wives as their own bodies. He that loveth his wife loveth himself. For no man ever yet hated his own flesh; but nourisheth and cherisheth it, even as the Lord the church: For we are members of his body, of his flesh, and of his bones. For this cause shall a man leave his father and mother, and shall be joined unto his wife, and they two shall be one flesh. This is a great mystery: but I speak concerning Christ and the church. Nevertheless let every one of you in particular so love his wife even as himself; and the wife *see* that she reverence *her* husband.

ROUTINES

As husbands, we have a tremendous responsibility. Sometimes we take this responsibility lightly and not in light of God's word. God was the one who instituted marriage in the beginning. Since He was the one that instituted it, He is the one that can fix it and keep it fixed. The single, most important event to ever happen in our marriage was when we dedicated our lives to the Lord in November 1991. That took place in the City of Refuge Christian Church in Hawaii. It not only changed our lives but it changed how we viewed marriage.

Routines can be good and bad. It is good when you routinely pray, seek God's guidance, study the Word of God, attend church, etc. However, it can be bad when you make your marriage "routine." For example: Monday through Friday, get up, shower, catch the news while dressing, grab a bagel, kiss her on the lips or cheek, go to work, back home, change, eat, shower, sleep, and no conversation. It happens unintentionally most of the time, but nevertheless it can happen. Avoid letting your relationship become routine.

Avoid the “routine” by viewing your marriage as God views it. God said that the husband and wife shall be one flesh. He also said that no man ever hated his own flesh. Let God change or enhance your attitude toward your wife. Begin viewing your marriage as a blessing from the Lord in which you can continuously reap benefits. Begin to thank God daily for your wife.

Pray and ask God to help you view marriage as He does. Ask God to show you what is most important, her inner-beauty. If your marriage needs fixing or just minor adjustments, ask Him for help. If you do not have a personal relationship with God or your marriage is not where it should be, ask Him for forgiveness and give Him control of your life.

Start this week by making it a habit of surprising her with flowers or something that you know will really please her. Do it because you truly love her and want her to know it.

THE SHEPHERD

Most of us are familiar with Psalm 23:1 (KJV) where David says, ***"The Lord is my Shepherd, I shall not want."*** As people, husbands fall into one of five categories: The Lord is their shepherd, The Lord will be their shepherd, The Lord was their shepherd, The Lord never was their shepherd, and The Lord never will be their shepherd. The right category to be in is that the Lord is your shepherd. Webster defines a shepherd as "one who herds sheep." More importantly, the characteristics of a shepherd include one who saves (willing to give his own life for another), protects, feeds, nourishes, shelters, displays loving care, provides, etc. You get the idea. Do you display these characteristics toward your wife? You cannot take the Lord's place in her life, but can she look to you as a shepherd? Can she say you provide "all that she needs?" Can she depend on you for spiritual and emotional nourishment? Is she worrying about how things are going to get done? The list could go on. You are a form of shepherd, whether you do a good or bad job. You can be a good shepherd to her by allowing the Lord to be your shepherd. It takes the "Good Shepherd" to teach you how to be a good shepherd.

Examine your ways, thoughts, and motives. Are they in line with God's Word? Pray and ask God to teach and empower you to be a good shepherd towards your wife.

Bless her by taking an active approach in handling and resolving those situations and problems that prevent her from having peace of mind and peace in the home.

SILENCE IS GOLDEN

This is a true statement when we are enjoying our quiet time, reading, praying, or meditating on God's Word, just to name a few. Temporary silence can be good in marriages when we are too angry to express ourselves properly and respectfully. Extended silence in marriage (lack of communication) can be and often is dangerous. We often get silent when we are angry. Anger is a natural and useful human emotion when used properly. Anger can provoke you to correct a situation. For example, if there is a lot of overspending in the home each month, anger could provoke you to establish and maintain a budget. Husbands and wives must keep the lines of communication open. There is a right way to present your concerns. They should not be presented in a threatening, manipulative, or one-way manner. Don't attack the wife; however; address the attitude or behavior that you perceive to be the problem. Sometimes it's just a perception. If you simply refuse to talk, it builds up within you until you over-react during a minor situation. If you deal with anger quickly and appropriately, you will not give the enemy the opportunity to magnify it and drive a wedge between the two of you. Ephesians 4:26-27 (NIV) says it best, ***"In your anger do not sin. Do not let the sun go down while you are still angry, and do not give the devil a foothold."***

Add kind words to your vocabulary and use them as necessary. Use phrases such as: I'm sorry, I was wrong, I made a mistake, please forgive me, I misunderstood, I love you, etc. Don't bring up old arguments.

Bless your wife by taking the lead in resolving problems. Turn problems and difficult situations into something positive for the marriage by drawing closer than ever to God and each other.

TEMPTATIONS

As much as you may want to be "one," often there are hindrances in fulfilling that desire. They are called temptations. Temptations come in many different shapes, sizes, ages, and colors. There is a temptation out there just for you. It's waiting for you to give it a second look or take hold of it. What might tempt you, may not interest the next person in any way. For example, if your interest is in poodles, a bulldog probably won't catch your attention (unless he's not on a leash). One of the problems with these temptations is that they have a tendency to just pop in your view. This happens at work, driving down the street, watching television, etc. Some call it "just admiring God's creations." Others say, "It's okay to look, as long I don't touch." Either of these thoughts or attitudes can and will eventually get you in trouble. Soon admiring and looking won't be enough. It moves to casual conversation. Then it starts moving like a freight train – very hard to stop. Temptations will come, but what's important is how you deal with it.

First Corinthians 10:12-13 (NIV) says, ***"So if you think you are standing firm, be careful that you don't fall! No temptation has seized you except what is common to man. And God is faithful; he will not let you be tempted beyond what you can bear. But when you are tempted, he will also provide a way out so that you can stand up under it."***

Being tempted is not the problem. The problem is when you don't handle it properly. God will provide the way for you to escape – ***RECOGNIZE IT AND TAKE IT!***

Bless your wife by staying true and devoted to her.

THE WALL

What wall? Is there a wall? How did it get there? It's not my wall; it's hers! Who made it?

Walls are normally upright structures designed to enclose, divide, support, or protect. So you can see how walls are good and bad. Walls in marriages are amazing. They are often invisible, yet if she gets too close, she will walk right into them. They are often in the front seat of the car on the way to church, and as you walk in the church they disappear and reappear as you get back in the car. The other amazing thing about these walls is that we can choose whether they will exist or not. You can decide with your attitude. Because we have so many responsibilities as husbands we often handle things without much effort. But there are times when persistent situations come up. We don't talk about it; we just keep pondering over it. Because our wives know us so well, they see it on our face, in how we treat them, and how we treat the children. Conversation goes to zero. Problems on the job should stay on the job. When you come home from work, check your attitude. Are you still upset about something at the office, a project, the boss, money, traffic, etc.? Have the attitude that regardless of what's going on, you have so many things to be thankful for. One of them is your wife who's waiting to see you when you come home.

When you come home and the door opens make sure she knows that she is the most important person on your mind. Let her know you missed her, give her a real kiss and not a peck (a hug wouldn't hurt either). Instead of unloading your troubles, ask her about her day. Ask God to help you and strengthen you. Ask Him to guide you and show you how to handle each situation, be it small or large. Ask God for a hedge of protection around your family. He wants to help. It doesn't matter who built the wall in your marriage, tear it down. Remember that it's your marriage.

Bless her by increasing the communication between the two of you. Let her know your concerns and ask her to pray with you (touch and agree). The attitude you come home with will (most likely) be the attitude she goes to bed with.

THE THIEF

I don't think any one of us would sit back and let a thief break into our car or house and not do anything about it. We would not let him take what he wanted and destroy everything else. We would at least call the police. The Bible warns us that there is a thief and he comes only to steal, kill and destroy (John 10:10a). He will try it in our lives and in our marriages, to name a few. He will attempt to ***steal*** intimacy, joy, and peace. He will attempt to ***kill*** all trust, communication, and kindness. He will attempt to ***destroy*** our love, faith, and ultimately our marriages.

But there is good news! Although we are warned that there is a thief and we are told what he plans to do, that's not the end of the story. There is help. Jesus has already come so that we may have life and have it to the fullest (John 10:10b). A marriage with life is centered on its Creator and our Heavenly Father. A marriage with life is full of love, communication, joy, peace, intimacy, etc.

Recognize that the enemy does exist and that he is effective in what he does only if we let him. More importantly, realize that God does exist. He is All Powerful and All Knowing (never caught off guard).

Before the thief presents himself, ask God for His divine favor and protection. Always make sure the house is secure and that your Queen is comfortably in bed before you get in bed and go to sleep.

CONFORM Vs TRANSFORM

When placed in a certain environment, our human nature is to conform (or adapt) to the prevailing opinion. We all live in a world that is harsh toward marriages and the family. Take just about any TV show and you can see what the media wants to shove in our brains about marriages. It seems that the prevailing opinion in the world about marriage is that it's not sacred, it's not forever, it's not necessarily between a man and a woman, it's not necessary, and if there are irreconcilable differences – that's a good reason to end it. Some say, "Everybody else is doing it." Just because everybody else is doing it, that doesn't make it right. There are some things we cannot accept without question. It's great to have harmony and peace, but when it violates what God says, that is where we need to draw the line. Romans 12:2 (NIV) says ***"Do not conform to the patterns of this world, but be transformed by the renewing of your mind. Then you will be able to test and approve what God's will is - his good, pleasing, and perfect will."*** Refuse to be influenced by societal pressures. If necessary, replace the old way of thinking and adopt a new perspective (God's point of view). In God's point of view, marriage is sacred, forever, and between one man and one woman. When there are differences, ask God to help you work it out.

Commit yourself to God and to your wife. If you have conformed or are considering conforming to the world's way, ask God to renew your mind and give you His perspective.

A wife has a way of knowing (probably a God-given ability) if the husband is totally committed to her. Love must be sincere.

Let your commitment to her be known and obvious. When she knows it, you will definitely see a difference. If she already knows it, you know what I'm writing about.

UNFAILING LOVE

When we were younger and thought we were truly in love, the girls would play a simple game to determine if the guy they admired loved them. She would pick a flower, such as a daisy, and begin plucking petals. "He loves me, he loves me not; he loves me, he loves me not; he loves me, he loves me not; he loves me, he loves me not...." This would continue until the last petal told her he does or does not love her. I guess the point here is that our wives should not have to still play this kind of game - day after day, week after week, month after month, year after year. Wives need security in their marriages. Love is consistent. There are three things which love can be based on:

Love 1 is "I love you because you do this for me."

Love 2 is "I will love you if you do or buy this for me."

Love 3 is "I love you regardless."

If you display love 1 (based on material things) or love 2 (manipulative), they are not consistent. You are not committed and you are double-minded. In the book of James chapter 1 verse 8, God lets us know that a double-minded man is unstable in all of his ways. There are situations that will come up in a marriage that will truly test the love you have for your wife. Since it is a test, you must pass it to get beyond it.

Love never fails (1 Corinthians 13:8a NIV).

Don't be double-minded in your love and commitment towards your wife. Eliminate the guesswork in your marriage (he loves me, he loves me not).

Let your love be consistent and enduring. Love her regardless.

VALENTINE

During this season the symbol of the heart seems to be most popular. It's a symbol that attempts to show our love, how we really feel toward that special someone. In another sense, the heart itself is considered the center of our emotions, our personal attributes, and our innermost thoughts and feelings. Some of us have experienced all or most of the various heart conditions, such as: heartache, heartburn, heart break, a change of heart, a hardness of heart, a clean heart, or even an unclean heart. Tough situations in life can fill your heart with all sorts of junk (bitterness, anger, hatred, prejudices, etc.).

If your heart is not where it should be, there is a solution. You can ask God to create in you a clean heart and renew a right spirit within you (Psalm 51). Romans 5:5 lets us know that it is the love of God that should be in our hearts.

Valentine's Day is coming. I'm reminding everybody early, because some men have a tendency to wait until the last minute to buy the card, flowers, candy, etc. Take some time and really think of a special, affordable way you and your wife (sweetheart) can enjoy this time together.

Here are some simple suggestions, in no particular order (there are enough for the whole month of February):

- Celebrate the entire month
- Celebrate the entire week
- Celebrate the 13 days leading up to Valentine's Day
- Cook dinner for the two of you (If child care is a problem, feed them early and put them to bed)

- Bring her red roses, carnations, etc.
- Bring her a heart-shaped box of candy
- Make reservations and have dinner at a nice restaurant
- Spend a romantic night at home
- Spend a romantic night at a nice hotel
- Get her a card
- Get her some jewelry (diamonds, gold, pearls, watch, bracelet, necklace, gemstones, etc.)
- Get her some perfume
- Get her a dress
- Get her some shoes
- Take her shopping
- Get her some lingerie
- Write her love notes each day from the 1st to the 13th, then something special on the 14th
- Breakfast in bed
- Write her a poem
- Get her a cake
- Take the day off and spend it with her
- Write her a letter with the 14 top reasons you love her
- Get her a personal gift (not something for the House)
- Give her a certificate for a massage by you
- Give her a gift certificate from her favorite store
- Let her get her hair, nails, etc. done
- Let her sleep in late
- If she has to work, have flowers delivered
- Bring home dinner
- Call her every hour, on the hour to tell her just how special she is to you
- Buy her a teddy bear or better yet, be her teddy bear

A BLESSED FOUNTAIN

"May your fountain be blessed, and may you rejoice in the wife of your youth." (Proverbs 5:18 NIV). Your wife may not like the idea of being referred to as a fountain. However, when you look at the significance of a fountain you can see that the reference compliments. A fountain can be viewed as a natural or artificial source of living and flowing water. Imagine how important and valuable a simple fountain can be in a dry and barren land. A fountain sustains life, even in a marriage. Although we live in a harsh world, our fountains can bring peace and soothing tranquillity. A blessed fountain (wife) is one that satisfies, refreshes, and provides pleasure. A blessed fountain (wife) is bubbling and overflowing with love within the marriage. A blessed fountain (wife) demonstrates and exercises unlimited ways to be all that her husband needs and more. She seeks ways to make the home his palace. A blessed fountain (wife) will make you only want to drink from her. A blessed fountain (wife) will cause you to rejoice without any hesitation. You will be proud to say, "This is my Wife, my Queen, my Sweetheart, my one-and-only." Her waters are sweet. A truly blessed fountain is one that has an intimate and personal relationship with God. God is the one and only source that empowers the wife to be the partner, friend, and lover that she is called to be. If your fountain (wife) is blessed, you are blessed and have reason to rejoice.

Bless her by encouraging her to be that blessed fountain. If she is not connected to the source that empowers her with spiritual strength and Godly wisdom, you lead the way and set the example.

BITTER WATERS

After Moses and the children of Israel crossed the Red Sea and had rejoiced in the defeat of their pursuers, the Egyptians, they went into the desert. They traveled for three days finding no water. When they did find water, it was so bitter they could not drink it. So they named the place "Marah," which means bitter or bitterness. Then the people began to grumble and complain. (Exodus 15:22-27). You can have great deliverance and victories in your life, but without drinkable water, life can come to a screeching halt. Perhaps your fountain is not as blessed as it should be. Maybe your fountain has plenty of water, but because of the past or because of sin it is now unbearable. Looking for another well or fountain is not the answer. Use Moses' experience as an example. ***"Then Moses cried out to the Lord, and the Lord showed him a piece of wood. He threw it into the water, and the water became sweet" (Exodus 15:25 NIV).*** Moses did exactly as he should have, he cried out to God. He prayed to God. God gave him the solution to the problem, and he was obedient. Moses was able to pray and hear God because he had a personal relationship with Him. Some may say it was the tree, others may say it was God's power alone that sweetened the waters. Either way, it shows us that if things with our wells are not the way they should be, we need to take it to God who can make a difference. God and God alone can truly soften hard hearts, sweeten the bitter waters in marriages, and make us new creations in Christ.

There are several things that can make your fountain (wife) produce bitter waters, but there is only One that can sweeten, restore, and bless your fountain.

Bless her by allowing God's love to flow through you to keep your fountain blessed and the waters it produces for you sweet.

YOUR OWN WELL

"Drink waters out of thine own cistern, and running waters out of thine own well." (Proverbs 5:15 KJV). A cistern is nothing more than a receptacle used for holding water. In the early days, cisterns were usually large pits with a small mouth. These pits were dug into the earth or rock. The mouth was covered with a flat rock, then with sand to prevent it from being discovered by others. In those days, wells and cisterns were privately owned and of great value. Just in case you have not figured it out, thine own well is "your own wife." Your wife should be your one and only source of intimate pleasure (not movies, not magazines, nor another woman). The Living Bible version makes it plain ***"Drink from your own well, my son – be faithful and true to your wife."*** Just as cool water will quench a man's thirst, let your wife and her alone meet your needs. Being faithful and true is more than just not going to bed with another woman. It also involves controlling your flesh (body). Don't let your eyes stray; looks are deceiving. With your ears, refuse to listen to the lustful call of another woman. Don't let anyone urge you to break your vows to God and your wife. Don't get intoxicated (in this case, with another woman's perfume). Once intoxicated, it is hard to make sound decisions and resist the temptations of the enemy. Don't let your feet carry you to another woman's house. Don't allow yourself to be in a situation where you are alone with another woman, even if you are "just friends." Don't let your mouth entice and invite another woman. Reserve your hands for your own wife. Lastly, don't let your mind wander.

Confine yourself to pleasures that are legitimately yours.

Bless her by being faithful and true, thus doing your part to keep your marital relationship **"pure."**

YOUR OWN WELL (II)

Just as wells and cisterns were privately owned, so is your wife. She is to be yours and yours alone. If you do not ***"Drink waters out of thine own cistern, and running waters out of thine own well." (Proverbs 5:15 KJV),*** you are asking for the consequences of verse 16 which continues by stating, ***"Should your springs overflow in the streets, your streams of water in the public squares."*** Since your wife should be your one and only source of intimate pleasure, you have a marital duty to your wife and she has the same to you. Her body is not hers alone and your body is not yours alone. You belong to each other. Therefore sex should not be intentionally withheld from each other out of anger and spite. Don't deprive each other of sexual fulfillment. If you deprive your wife of normal sexual activity, she may be tempted to take what is private and let it overflow in the streets (in public).

There are times when restraint from normal intimacy is necessary, but it should be with the consent of both the husband and wife. Please see 1 Corinthians 7:3-5. Just because her body is yours also, that doesn't mean you can hop on and satisfy your desires when and where you want. Be considerate.

On the subject of overflowing in public we have to consider how she dresses. As stated in the previous lesson, the mouth of a well or cistern was covered with a flat rock, then with sand to prevent it from being discovered by others. I think this speaks directly to the way the wife dresses. Everybody she meets should not know what her body looks like because her clothes are so revealing. No need to go into specific details, I think you know what I mean. She can look good without everybody else knowing the details.

That which is private, keep it private.

Bless her by meeting her needs and by being considerate.

SATISFIED AND CAPTIVATED

"A loving doe, a graceful deer – may her breasts satisfy you always, may you ever be captivated by her love (Proverbs 5:19 NIV)." May your wife be ***as*** kind, tender, pleasant, attractive, and graceful as a delicately beautiful doe. In the beginning, God created the woman from man and for man. Adam was definitely satisfied and captivated by Eve's beauty. I guess the question is, are you satisfied? Her body is to satisfy you and only you, forever. God created sex for at least three purposes. They are to provide children, pleasure, and intimacy. Only God can create one thing and cause it to serve several divine purposes. He could have chosen to let sex be purely for the purpose of providing children. But He thought of the husband and wife and their need also for pleasure and intimacy. Everything that God created was good or very good. Sin has caused sex to be viewed as dirty, nasty, or as a bargaining tool. The problem comes when one tries to be satisfied with a person who is not their spouse; one ends up getting taken captive or entangled. The idea is for the husband and wife to be virtually intoxicated with each other's love. This "intoxication" is not like getting drunk because that type eventually wears off and leaves you with a hangover. Rather, it's a feeling of wild excitement for her. An excitement that doesn't wear off, get old, fade, or leave you with a hangover.

There is new inner-beauty, pleasure, and intimacy yet to be discovered within her. Don't stop searching.

Bless her by letting her know that you are very much satisfied with her and excited about her.

A DRY WELL

Often we take things for granted, such as fresh air, pure water, good health, etc. There is a saying that "you don't miss your water until your well runs dry," because for most of us, water always seems to be there when we need it. We don't think twice about using it to shower, cook, water the lawn, have a water fight, or to quench a thirst. Let's not take our wives for granted. They are a significant part of our lives. They make us complete. Perhaps you feel that the well of your marriage is running dry. You know, the excitement doesn't seem to be there any more. The joy is not as strong that used to fill your heart when you knew you would see her soon after a brief but necessary separation. The intimate moments are few and far between. It's hard to even have casual conversations. So what do you do? For starters, don't discard the well. Dig deeper, and try harder. Don't ever feel that you don't need her. That would be like saying, "I don't need my heart or lungs any longer. Don't let your well run dry before you realize the significance and necessity of your well of water. Usually people run out of water because they waste it and not value it. Fortunately, love (Godly love) is not like water. It never ceases. ***"May your fountain be blessed, and may you rejoice in the wife of your youth" (Proverbs 5:18 NIV).***

Make sure your wife knows that you appreciate her. Make it a habit of letting her know you appreciate everything she does, even the small things.

Bless her with the kind words and compliments that come only from the heart, a heart filled with the Love of God.

THE LAST ONE

No, this is not the last lesson. However, when there is an abundance of something or it is readily available, we take it for granted. What were the last words you spoke to your wife? Were they words of encouragement, words of deceit, or words of anger? What was the last kiss like? Was it a peck on the cheek or was it a passionate one? What was the last intimate moment like? Was it just a moment? Was it more like a "Hit and run accident," or was it memorable, satisfying, and exciting? What was the day like? Was it a day of joy or was it a day of bitterness and resentment? I ask these questions because we never know when one of these events will be the last one. Since we have no idea when the last kiss, hug, day, or words spoken will be, we should treat each occasion as it possibly being the last one. If you knew when the last kiss would be, it would probably last for an hour before either came up for air. If you knew when the last time you would be able to speak to your wife, you would ensure the words were sweet, kind, compassionate, forgiving, and loving. If tonight were the last chance for an intimate time together, you wouldn't put it off or be too tired; rather, you would make each moment pleasurable and completely satisfying. You would go out of your way to please her. Therefore, enjoy, have fun, and treat each moment as though it could be the last.
"...Rejoice with the wife of thy youth" (Proverbs 5:18b KJV).

Enjoy each other to the fullest. Put each other's needs before your own. This makes for fewer regrets later. Realize that every day is a day that the Lord has made, rejoice and be glad in each one!

Bless her by making your time together pleasant, memorable, and without regrets.

BEING ONE

In the natural, "being one" is a mystery. Ephesians 5:28, 29 (NIV) (in part) says, ***"...husbands ought to love their wives as their own bodies. He who loves his wife loves himself. After all, no one ever hated his own body, but he feeds and cares for it, just as Christ does the church."*** Normal people take good care of themselves, but there are some who abuse their bodies with drugs, cigarettes, neglect, etc. Those are the exceptions, rather than the rule. When a husband and wife are one, they complement and compliment each other. To *Complement,* is to make complete or bring to perfection. The two of you are just what is needed to make a complete set. You make her complete, and she makes you complete. As a matter of fact, you just downright look good together. To *Compliment,* is to show an act of courtesy toward each other. Be the first one to praise your wife for how beautiful she looks and for the things she does. If you don't do it, someone else will.

Being one is not just while being intimate, although intimacy is one of God's gifts and a perfect example of being perfectly joined. Being one is how you carry and present yourself even when you are out alone shopping, in the grocery store, at the barbershop, hanging with the guys, etc. You are one even when you are at work and she is at home because of the bonding that has already taken place and because of your commitment to your wife.

God Loves You! We should love the things that God loves and hate the things that He hates. Because He loves **you**, love yourself, not self-centeredly, but love yourself as someone that God created and designed. Realize that God created you uniquely for His purpose.

Bless your wife by loving yourself. You will have no problem truly loving your wife (because she is part of you).

ONE + ONE = ONE

Adam said: ***"This is now bone of my bones and flesh of my flesh; she shall be called Woman, because she was taken out of Man." Therefore a man shall leave his father and mother and be joined to his wife, and they shall become one flesh (Genesis 2:23,24).*** God put Adam into a deep sleep and took one of Adam's ribs and made Woman. He made a "helper" that was suitable to man in every way (mentally, physically, spiritually, emotionally, and socially). So naturally Adam was excited about his companion. Women are not inferior; Adam acknowledged her as equal (bone of my bones and flesh of my flesh). So what about a man leaving his father and mother? The success of your marriage is on your shoulders. Fathers and mothers may offer advice and assistance, but you are ultimately responsible for your marriage and taking care of the family. The responsibility for keeping your marriage together is also on your shoulders. The Amplified Bible says that ***"...A man must leave his father and mother when he marries, so that he can be perfectly joined to his wife, and the two shall be one" (Ephesians 5:31 AMP).*** When a husband and wife are perfectly joined, there is completeness. In order to be perfectly joined, your dependency should not be on your parents. Your dependency should be on Christ, and He should be the bonding factor.

Focus on doing those things that will bring you closer to being "perfectly joined" to your wife.

Bless your wife by allowing her to be the companion and partner that she was designed and created (by God) to be for you.

PERFECTLY JOINED

In Psalm 139:13-14 (NIV), David the psalmist writes ***"For you created my inmost being; you knit me together in my mother's womb. I praise you because I am fearfully and wonderfully made; your works are wonderful, I know that full well."*** Have you ever thought about how perfectly the different parts of your body work together? When you are hungry your stomach will quickly tell you it is time to eat. As a matter of fact, your stomach will give you advance warning, before it's time to eat. Have you ever had to tell your lungs to breathe? Have you ever had to tell your heart to beat? Each part of our body instinctively works together to do what it is supposed to do. That is because God created us that way. One part of the body cannot survive by itself. If you stump your toe, the whole body will know it in less than a second. Being perfectly joined to your wife makes you promptly aware of her hurts, concerns, desires, etc. Your brain is sensitive to the body's needs so it takes charge by issuing commands to the other parts of the body to do their job. Just as the brain is sensitive to the body, you must be sensitive to your wife and to the marriage as a whole. Just as the brain is aware that a part of the body hurts, you should know when your wife hurts, needs more attention, or just needs some quiet time. That is just how close husbands and wives should be.

Realize that you and your wife are perfectly joined in a supernatural way. Therefore, be cognizant of what is going on in your marriage and be sensitive to her needs.

Bless your wife by letting her know that you really do care.

BURDENS

Imagine you are going for a long walk by yourself with a large backpack. In your backpack you have two huge car payments, a large mortgage, several over-the-limit credit cards, three rebellious teenagers, a sick child, and a nagging wife. As you start to walk, the load seems pretty heavy, but you are determined it will be okay. A gentleman walks up beside you with a small bag and asks to carry your load for you. You reply, "No, I'm a man, I can handle it." So you speed up your walk to get some distance from the gentleman. By now you are really struggling with this load. The gentleman catches up to you again and says, "You're going my way, how about I carry your large back pack and you carry my small bag?"

Believe it or not there is someone who wants to help you with your burdens. In fact He said ***"Come to me, all you who are weary and burdened and I will give you rest. Take my yoke upon you and learn from me, for I am gentle and humble in heart, and you will find rest for your souls. For my yoke is easy and my burden is light (Matthew 11:28-30 NIV)."***

Marriage does come with concerns, don't let them become worries. Sometimes we attempt to handle the small problems ourselves and pray about the large ones, or we attempt to handle them all ourselves. Remember, a ton of feathers and a ton of bricks weigh the same.

If marriage has thrown you some unexpected curve balls, it takes a big man to admit he needs help, and it takes a bigger man to ask for help. Jesus has made us all an offer that we should not refuse. He wants us to have rest and peace. Let's cast all our cares (large and small) upon Him, for He cares for us. ***"Do not be anxious about anything, but in everything, by prayer and petition, with thanksgiving, present your requests to God. And the peace of God which transcends all understanding, will guard your hearts and your minds in Christ Jesus. (Philippians 4:6-7 NIV)"***

Bless your wife by getting rid of the humongous backpack and burdens. You'll then be able get around a whole lot easier.

COMMANDMENT

I think that all of the guidance, instruction, wisdom, etc. to husbands can be summed up into one phrase. I view this phrase as a commandment specifically for the husband. It is not directed at all men, nor is it directed at women at all. However, women (wives) are the receivers of the action. If the husband can truly do this, he in fact will do all that God wants him to do in his relationship with his wife. So how can you do all that God wants you to do in your relationship with your wife? The phrase (commandment) is simply "Husbands, love your wives." It's a powerful statement. I know you feel that you have been doing it for years and got it covered. God not only tells us what to do, but how to do it. He sets a goal for us to strive for. The goal is Ephesians 5:25-33 (NIV) "*...**just as Christ loved the church and gave himself up for her to make her holy, cleansing her by the washing with water through the word, and to present her to himself as a radiant church, without stain or wrinkle or any other blemish, but holy and blameless. In this same way, husbands ought to love their wives as their own bodies. He who loves his wife loves himself. After all, no one ever hated his own body, but he feeds and cares for it, just as Christ does the church - for we are members of his body. "For this reason a man will leave his father and mother and be united to his wife, and the Two will become one flesh." This is a profound mystery - but I am talking about Christ and the church. However, each one of you also must love his wife as he loves himself, and the wife must respect her husband."***

- Are you willing to die for her? Rather, are you willing to live a Godly life for her?

- Are you taking the steps necessary to ensure that you both make it to Heaven?
- Are you united as one?
- Are you loving her as you love yourself? (exercise, healthy food, nice attire, rest, etc.)
- Is your intimacy for her deepening each day

Be a blessing to your wife by putting her spiritual, emotional, physical, security, and fulfillment needs at the same level or above your own.

THE "D" WORD

I would much rather be writing about "Darling," "Dedicated," "Devoted," etc., but there is another word that keeps coming up in marriages everywhere. Okay, here it is, I have to say it – "divorce." When most of us got married it was in a church with a man of God, such as a priest, pastor, or reverend officiating the ceremony. We recited the words of the preacher, dedicating ourselves to each other forever. Further stating, "until death do us part." Then, to top it off, the preacher seals it with, "What God has joined together, let not man put asunder (separate)." Why is it that people go to God to get married and go to man (courts) for divorce? Why not go back to God and see what he has to say about it? Why are people divorcing for every reason under the sun?

I'm not saying that under no circumstance should divorce be granted, but it should not be the first, second, or even the third option that comes to mind. Initial options should include praying, repentance, forgiveness, temporary separation, counseling, deliverance, etc. God only allowed divorce in the first place because of the hardness of man's heart.

Eliminate the "D" word from your vocabulary. Ban it from being used in your home. Realize that there are better options for resolving disputes in your marriage.

Bless your wife by living your original marriage vows. Consider renewing your vows in church, before God, and friends.

LOVE FORGIVES

You've heard the saying that "Love is never having to say you are sorry." In my opinion, "Love is being able to say you are sorry." At some point or another in marriage, the need to say "I'm sorry" or "I forgive you" will come. When you make a mistake or hurt someone you love, love will make you say I'm sorry, I apologize, or please forgive me. Love, in turn, will also make the one that was hurt willing to forgive. Love wants the relationship mended. Asking for forgiveness and granting forgiveness heals relationships. The sooner it is done the less bitterness that will build up. In Ephesians 4:31,32, (NIV) the Word of God tells us to ***"Get rid of all bitterness, rage, and anger, brawling and slander along with every form of malice. [and] Be kind and compassionate to one another, forgiving each other, just as in Christ God forgave you."*** Bitterness, rage, and anger not properly dealt with will quickly end a marriage. However, kindness, compassion, and forgiveness will go a long way in creating a lasting marital relationship.

If you don't ask for forgiveness or grant forgiveness, it will put you and the relationship in bondage, unable to function as you should, unable to grow closer. Be quick to ask for and give forgiveness.

Bless your wife by letting love cover many wrongs.

A MASTERPIECE

Yes, you are married to "A Masterpiece!" She is unique, original, and one-of-a-kind! There is no one else on Earth like her. She was uniquely made and formed by the skills of not only a master, but by the "Master" himself. Some of God's greatest work was when He fashioned Woman. In Psalm 139:13-14 (NIV), David the psalmist writes ***"For you created my inmost being; you knit me together in my mother's womb. I praise you because I am fearfully and wonderfully made; your works are wonderful, I know that full well."*** God is involved in every detail of our lives, not just our formation. There are millions and millions of women in the world, but not a single one is exactly like your wife. Cherish the fact that your wife is an original work of art. Owners of masterpieces often just sit around and admire the beauty, knowing that there is not another one around. I guess that makes your wife, just like mine, "absolutely priceless." Over time, the value and worth of a masterpiece always increases. The owner of a masterpiece will insure it and risk his life for it. Even if you don't think your wife is a masterpiece, God does. John 3:16 (KJV) says it well, ***"For God so loved the world, that He gave his only begotten Son, that whosoever believeth in him should not perish, but have everlasting life."*** God was and is still serious about the value and worth of each one of us. Take very good care of the "Masterpiece" that God has placed in your care.

Realize what you have. Admire her as a true work of art made especially for you and no one else.

Cherish her by showing her love, protection, and tender care.

A ROLE MODEL MARRIAGE

My friend and his wife recently celebrated 20 years of marriage together on March 22. I gave my congratulations to them both. Although they have been married to each other for 20 years, it doesn't mean it was all "a bed of roses." However, it does mean that they endured, they were forgiving, and they considered the needs of their partner. Today, it seems as though couples have very little endurance, very low tolerance, and no mercy or forgiveness. I applaud everyone that is determined to make his or her marriage work. The young couples today need you and the example that you present. You may never know the impact that you have on other couples. We often complain about the rising number of divorces, but what are we doing about it. Your marriage is important and you can make a difference. Your sons, daughters, and acquaintances are looking and observing how you treat your wife. They don't expect nor will they see a perfect marriage. But they do need to see a marriage that effectively handles differences and quickly overcomes obstacles by trusting in God. If each of us will be that good example, we can definitely make a difference. Remember, 1 John 3:18 (KJV), ***"My little children, let us not love in word, neither in tongue; but in deed and in truth."*** It is good and also easy to write and say "I love you," but the test is to let your actions speak for you.

Whether you have been married one day, six months, five years, twenty years, or more – be a positive marriage role model! If you ask, God can and will help.

Bless your wife by letting your deeds speak louder than your words.

OFF LIMITS

We have grown accustomed to the fact that certain places and things are simply "Off-Limits." Our scripture asks a simple question – "Why?" "***Why be captivated, my son, by an adulteress? Why embrace the bosom of another man's wife?" (Proverbs 5: 20 NIV)*** In light of the fact that God has given you a "Masterpiece," a wife that is unique and one-of-a-kind, why commit adultery? The problem with an adulteress is that her lips drip honey and her speech is smoother than oil (verse 3). She knows how to lay the sweet talk on very thick, she promises to be better than what you already have. She goes out of her way to be desirable and pleasant to the eyes. Her words are soothing and flattering. She will tell you just what you want to hear, such as, how big your muscles are and how handsome you are. She knows how to overlook your bad characteristics and highlight the good. ***"But in the end she is bitter gall, sharp as a double-edged sword. Her feet go down to death; her steps lead straight to the grave. She gives no thought to the way of life; her paths are crooked, but she knows it not." (Proverbs 5:4-6 NIV)*** Just as certain places are off-limits, so is another man's wife or a woman that is not your wife. One piece of advice is offered in verse 8 ***"Keep to a path far from her, do not go near the door of her house."***

If she is not your wife, view her as "off-limits."

Bless your wife by demonstrating the joy only found within the bonds of marriage.

PSST! PSST!

You are being watched! We all are! Not by aliens, but by an All-knowing, Almighty, Omnipresent, and loving God. Proverbs 5:21 (NIV) ***"For a man's ways are in full view of the Lord and He examines all his paths."*** Everything we do and every thought and intent of the heart is seen and known by God. We should appreciate the fact that God is watching our every move. We should take comfort in the fact that when we get in trouble He is already aware of the situation. It was God who said He would never leave us nor forsake us.

But there are some who don't appreciate God's omniscience. When it comes to lying, cheating, and stealing, some think that nobody knows. God knows. An extra-marital affair has a bit of excitement to it. The door is locked, the shades are pulled, the lights are out, it's hidden, and it's often done at night in the cover of darkness. What's more important to us is that it violates God's Holy standard. Hebrews 4:13 (NIV), makes it very plain, ***"Nothing in all creation is hidden from God's sight. Everything is uncovered and laid bare before the eyes of him to whom we must give account."***

Are you prepared to give account for each and every act, thought, and intent? This includes how you treat your wife. Is she treated as mere property, second class, or unimportant? Are you prepared for God to examine your paths?

To be on the "safe side," examine yourself; let your actions, thoughts, and intents of your heart be in line with God's Word.

If they are not,
1) acknowledge it to God,
2) ask Him to forgive you,
3) give Him full control over your life. Let God be the one who directs and establishes your steps.

Be true, open, and honest with your wife. Choose to live a Godly life.

DON'T BE ENVIOUS

Psalm 37:1 says, "Do not fret because of evil men or be envious of those who do wrong; for like the grass they will soon wither, like green plants they will soon die away." We often see evil or crooked things done that seem to be prosperous and make people famous. We see the majority of people going in a certain direction but deep down inside we know that what they are doing is unethical, ungodly, unlawful, selfish, or just plain cruel. They seem to get away with their wrongs. They may even live a long life and die wealthy. Sometimes the road less traveled is the right road to take. Just because everybody else is going in a certain direction does not make it right. Know where you are going, what it takes to get there, and don't take short cuts. Usually if it "sounds to good to be true," it usually is.

If your desire is to make it to Heaven, check the road that you are on. It may not be the easier route. As you travel, there may be only a few others on the same road. It has been said that "All roads lead to Rome," but Jesus said, ***(John 14:6 (NKJV) "I am the way, the truth, and the life. No one comes to the Father except through Me."*** Now you know who is the way (Jesus), you know who is the truth (Jesus), and you know who gives eternal life (Jesus).

If you are not on the road to Heaven you can start right here and now. First acknowledge that you have sinned by doing things your way instead of God's way. Then ask God for forgiveness. Next invite Jesus Christ into your heart. Accept Him as your Lord and Savior by accepting the redemptive work in His death, burial, and resurrection. By accepting Jesus Christ as Savior, you will have eternal life, and the promises of God to His people are yours!

If you want to love your wife as God intended, it starts with a close relationship with His Son. Those who are in Christ have no reason to be envious.

Bless your wife by loving her God's way.

WHO DO YOU KNOW?

As recorded in Genesis 2:23, (NIV) Adam said, ***"This is now bone of my bones and flesh of my flesh; she shall be called woman, for she was taken out of man." For this reason a man will leave father and mother and be united to his wife, and they will become one flesh."*** In Genesis 4:1 the scripture says, ***"And Adam knew (laid with, had sexual intercourse with) his wife Eve…."*** At this point they fulfilled Genesis 2:23 in becoming one flesh. Notice that Adam did not lay with Eve before she was his wife.

In one sense it is often helpful to know people in various places. You never know when you may need to call on someone for assistance. To ***know*** a woman, in the way Genesis 4:1 describes, means you have become one with that person. ***(Do you not know that he who unites himself with a prostitute [or any woman] is one with her in body? For it is said, "The two will become one flesh" 1 Corinthians 6:16).*** So how many women do you ***know*** or how many women did you ***know*** before you married? Don't answer. Most of us ***know*** more women than we care to admit. Whether you know her name or not, something significant happened – the two of you became one. That event is now etched in your mind. It may often, occasionally, or never flash across your mind, but the fact remains that it happened. So how do you deal with this now that you are settled with the wife you have? Psychiatrists, therapists, or lawyers cannot sever this hold that this event has on you. Only genuine repentance (to the True and Living God, who is willing and able to thoroughly forgive and cleanse) is the answer. David ***knew*** Bathsheba, a woman who was not his wife, but he also, more importantly ***knew a merciful God.***

If this is you, use Psalm 51, written by David, as a model prayer for mercy, washing, cleansing, purging, and restoration and let **God create in you a pure heart!**

Bless your wife by sharing your new, pure heart only with her.

PRIORITIES

A soldier's priority (commitment) is to the United States, the U.S. Army, the unit and it's mission, soldiers, and families. However, there are priorities greater than these. As Christians, our number one priority is God, our relationship with His Son Jesus, and His Holy Spirit. If there is a proper relationship with Jesus, you will have a proper relationship with the church. Next, is our family (wife, children, and parents). We have a natural desire to excel and be successful in this society. In the process, we often get our priorities out of order and the end result is trouble with God. Although the order is established, balance is necessary. First check your relationship with God, and then ask God what is His advice and guidance in the situations and tests you are going through. One key point is that tests will come, and they will show you where your priorities lie. Remember that it is a "test." As with tests in the natural, either you pass or fail. If you fail, you usually have to retake the test. Retaking the test means more studying, more heartache, and more endurance and patience. So what you want to do is to get through the test the first time. I probably don't know much about you and your spouse personally, but one thing about life's tests is that all of the answers are already provided in God's Word. As the head of your home, you are responsible to God for all that goes right and all that goes wrong. As the husband, you have to identify the "bottom-line problem," seek God's guidance and direction, then make your decision. No one can or should try to decide for you and God will not force you. The ideal marriage is to have a husband and wife who both love the Lord, with a husband who is a spiritual leader in the home and a wife who is submissive to her husband's leadership. If this is not the case, work with what you have (never give up on the marriage) and ask God to make it better. Lastly, a husband and wife being together is very important.

Check your priorities in life. Seek first the kingdom of God…(Matthew 6:33).

She will be blessed to know that your relationship with her is second only to your relationship with God.

SUBMISSION

"Wives, submit yourselves unto your own husbands, as unto the Lord (Ephesians 5:22)." This is one of those scriptures that has been misused and abused. The idea of submission is respect and being able to speak louder with a kind, respectful, and Christ-like behavior. In other words, be submissive and adaptive to your husband's leadership. If you mention this to most women today, they will surely call you a chauvinist (among other things). Needless to say, a submissive spirit runs counter to the world's view. We are encouraged to submit (yield in love) to one another out of reverence for Christ (Ephesians 5:21). Therefore husbands, if you expect your wife to be submissive to your leadership, then you need to be submissive and reverent to Christ as your Head. Wives have problems following husbands with no direction, goal, or vision. Just like in combat, soldiers are hesitant to follow a leader who has no idea what he is supposed to accomplish. Yes, there are limits to submission. Submission does not mean participating in sinful or questionable behavior. Being submissive to one another does not mean being a "door mat" either. Just respect one another because of who Christ is and for what He has done in our lives. Regardless of what society says, remember it remains God's standard for all believers, male and female, for all times.

Get your clear instructions from the Master Himself. By doing so, you can trust the guidance you get and your wife will be less hesitant to submit to your leadership.

Bless her by not taking advantage of her (abusing your authority), especially when she is being obedient to God's Word by being submissive to your leadership.

WHICH WAY ARE WE GOING?

Is this an unspoken question that wives are wondering? When it comes to reasons why it is difficult for a wife to submit (be subjective, submissive, adaptive) to her own husband, some of the main reasons are lack of leadership and direction.

Most women (wives) would enjoy the ease of letting the husband make the difficult decisions and take charge of situations. Although, wives would at least appreciate the opportunity to offer input and suggestions. But the problem is when husbands don't take charge. When wives see reluctance on the part of the husband to deal with a particular situation, they will take action. Leaders assess situations, seek guidance, gather information, and then make decisions. Sometimes this takes seconds, days, or even longer, dependent upon the situation. Leaders also take responsibility for their actions, especially when things go wrong.

Take the biblical account of Adam and Eve in the Garden of Eden (Genesis 3:1-13). We do not know if Adam was with Eve when she spoke to the serpent and took of the forbidden fruit. However, I believe the results would have been different if Adam would have took charge and simply told her "No" (if he was with her). If he was not with her, as soon as he realized what happened, he could have taken charge of the situation by not eating of the forbidden fruit and immediately leading her to ask God for forgiveness. Instead, he blamed Eve (the bone of his bones, flesh of his flesh), the wife that God gave him.

So remember that you are in a position of great responsibility, so take charge (in a loving and caring way).

When you apply the guidance and direction you get from God, her lack of trust will decrease and her willingness to submit will increase. Bless her by accepting your place of leadership in the marriage.

IN THE RIGHT ORDER

Husbands: Love your wives
Wives: Submit to your husbands
Children: Obey your parents
(Ephesians 5:22 through Ephesians 6:3)

God made it this way to establish order in the family and home. While we are all directed to submit to one another in the fear (reverence) of God, wives are further instructed to be submissive to their own husbands. Wives are not to be submissive to mankind (as inferior), but to their husband's leadership and authority. This is submission among equals; not saying that one is smarter or better than the other.

When a wife is not submissive to her husband, she is not provided that covering that God intended. For example, in the home, the wife may have certain authority. She may have authority to make certain decisions without consulting the husband. The husband has delegated this authority to the wife. However, when she makes a decision on a matter over which she has no authority to do, she has (in a sense) stepped outside of her authority and out from under her covering. When she makes a decision within her authority, she should have the husband's support. When she makes a decision outside of her authority, she violates the established order, which could cause disruption in the home and marriage. It's like the enemy has to go through the husband to get to the wife, but if the wife is not under her husband's covering she may be vulnerable to the enemy. So, ***"Be sober, be vigilant; because your adversary the devil walks about like a roaring lion, seeking whom (out-of-order marriages) he may devour (1 Peter 5:8 NKJV)."***

If the devil is after your wife, let him know that he has to come through you first and that you are not about to let it happen.

Bless your wife by providing her that covering and protection you, as the husband, have been charged to provide.

TWO-HEADED MONSTER

God did not create any two-headed monsters, but they have been in existence since the beginning of mankind. In two-headed marriages, the husband and wife may be "one" on certain things, but pulling in opposite directions on other things. Ephesians 5:22-24 sets the order in a marriage so that the two-headed monster syndrome will not flare up. ***"Wives, submit to your husbands as to the Lord. For the husband is the head of the wife as Christ is the head of the church, his body, of which he is Savior. Now as the church submits to Christ, so also wives should submit to their husbands in everything. (NIV)"*** [Submit in everything except sinful behavior.] If a church is not in line with the Word of God, then it is not submitting to Christ, it's Head. Unfortunately, there are churches where Christ is not the head. Christ does not force Himself as the head of a church. In other words, in order for the husband to be the head of the wife, she must be submissive, adaptive, and subject to her own husband. Being the Head is not a status the man should force upon the wife, rather she should yield herself out of reverence and love for her husband, just as she submits to Christ. In a lot of situations, two heads are better than one. It is great when two people can come together to find a workable solution. This works even in marriages. However, the husband is ultimately responsible because God has given him this authority and responsibility. Rebellion against the order that God has established is rebellion against God Himself.

Being head in the marriage does not mean you have got all the brains and wisdom.

Bless your wife by asking for her input and showing your appreciation for her point of view. Make the decision, accept responsibility, and give credit when and where it is due.

T-N-T

In other words, "Tough and Tender." Being tough is usually not a problem for men. It is in our nature to be tough and masculine. Even as a child we were taught to be tough and not to cry. So, for a man to be compassionate, it can be difficult. There is a time for toughness and a time for tenderness. Ephesians 4:32 (NIV), tells us to ***"Be kind and compassionate to one another, forgiving each other, just as in Christ God forgave you."*** As a reminder, this scripture also applies in the home and in the marriage.

We sometimes have a tendency to be kind, compassionate, and more forgiving to others (even strangers) than to our own spouses. Am I saying that we should be quick in showing kindness, compassion, and forgiveness toward our spouses? "Yes." God is, always has been, and will continue to be just, kind, compassionate, and forgiving toward us.

We should follow the examples that Jesus left for us. Jesus showed us both toughness and tenderness as He hung on the cross (paying the penalty for our sins). Jesus knew that the penalty for sin was death. Not once did He cry because of the pain. It took a tough person, to be innocent, yet willing to die, so others may live. Some of His final words on the cross were, "Father, forgive them, for they do not know what they are doing." Now that's "Tough and Tender." (If you haven't thanked Him for paying the penalty for your sins and accepted Him as your Lord and personal Savior, please do so right now.)

The quicker we forgive the quicker the healing and restoration begins. Don't let anger control us, rather, let's control our anger.

Bless your wife by being a "Tough-and-Tender" kind of husband.

A FEELING

There is a beautiful Christian song that says, "I've got a ***feeling***, everything's gonna be all right!" I would like to take it a step further and tell you that it's more than a feeling. We've got a ***promise***, everything's gonna be all right! Certain "feelings" have a tendency to come and go. Sometimes we feel like we can't make it and sometimes we feel we can conquer anything that comes our way. But we have promises from God. His promises are recorded in His Holy Word – the Bible. His promises of healing, deliverance, strength, peace, joy, etc. first start with our believing His promise of salvation to those who accept His Son Jesus as their personal Lord and Savior. Regardless of what you may be going through right now, He has promised that He will be right there with you – He will never leave you nor forsake you. You can't say that about anyone else. No one can compare to the faithfulness of God.

The marriage vows to your spouse were more than just a feeling; they were promises. They were lifetime commitments, through the best and worst of times. Believe in your spouse and your marriage. Be determined not to give up when the going gets rough. Depend on God's strength to get you through the struggles. When you are ready to give up and quit, remember that Jesus said, ***"If you can believe, all things are possible to him who believes. (Mark 9:23b NKJV)"***

We have promises from God; promises you can have faith in. I've heard it said, "If God said it, I believe it and that settles it." Bless your wife by being a "promise and marriage vow keeper."

A SECRET PLACE

Your relationship may or may not be going through a difficult time right now. There may be times of pressure, hurt, division, etc. You may not know what to do. But know that you can take your marriage (or any other situation) to a secret place. Do more than just take it there, let it remain there permanently. ***"He who dwells in the secret place of the Most High shall abide under the shadow of the Almighty (Psalm 91:1 NKJV)."*** He who takes up permanent residence in the shelter of God shall remain stable and firmly rooted under His awesome power. So how do you take up (permanent) residence in God's shelter? Residency starts by being in right standing with God, by constantly praying, and by being faithful to Him. When someone is outside and the temperature is very high, just a simple shadow from a tree or a building will provide almost instant relief from the sun. Relief may be easier to obtain than you think. Prayer and trust in God is your relief from all that the enemy may be sending your way.

This secret place is only secret from those who do not trust Him. You cannot trust Him if you don't know Him.

Bless your wife by being a praying husband. Take your marriage to "the secret place."

A SECRET PLACE (II)

Husbands and wives often take comfort in the fact that they have been married for years, live in nice neighborhoods, their houses are secure, their cars don't break down, the police are responsive, the hospital is close by, money is in the bank, and they have planned for the future. While these things are nice, they do not truly provide the peace, comfort, security, and rest we need. ***"He who dwells in the secret place of the Most High shall abide under the shadow of the Almighty (Psalm 91:1 (NKJV)."*** In His place, marriages will find rest under His awesome power. David found a Divine Refuge and Fortress. ***"I will say of the Lord, He is my refuge and my fortress; my God; in him will I trust. (v 2)"*** But the question remains, "What are you saying?" Are you proclaiming the Lord as your refuge and protector of your home and marriage? Are you proclaiming Him as your God? Is it He in whom you put your trust? Are you trying to take comfort and have security in material things? Our power and might is very limited. As much as we may desire security and peace in the marriage, there is only so much that we can do. That is why it is important to put it in God's hand, under His awesome power. Try saying to the Lord, "You are my God," (not money, my job, or my status) "In You and You alone Lord, do I put my trust." In the secret place, you will find all that you need and more.

The enemy is seeking marriages to destroy; however, he has no access to those firmly rooted and grounded in the secret place – God's refuge and fortress.

Bless your wife by trusting God to provide "Maximum, Super-Ultimate Marriage Protection."

WHAT'S IN IT FOR ME?

This is really the wrong attitude to have in a marriage. This is an attitude of selfishness and self-centeredness. The real danger comes when one of the marriage partners says, "There is nothing in this marriage for me." Instead of thinking only about self and having the attitude of get all you can get, try giving. Try placing her needs above your own. It is recorded in the Book of Acts, Chapter 20, verse 35 that Jesus said, ***"It is more blessed to give than to receive."*** In the Book of Luke, Chapter 6, verse 38, Jesus also instructs us to ***"Give, and it shall be given unto you…."*** It may be hard to grasp, but within the marriage, if you want love, try giving love. If you want peace, try being a peacemaker. If you want joy, try being joyful and pleasant. If you want faithfulness, try being faithful. If you want honesty, try being honest. If you want romance, try being romantic. This is not a guarantee, but do your part and let God do the rest.

Remember, you are no longer two, you are now one. Webster's New World Dictionary defines oneness as singleness; unity, unity of mind, feelings, etc. It is no longer "I," but "we."

Try sowing into the relationship what you would like to reap.

Be a blessing to your wife by practicing unity and oneness, and by sowing love and faithfulness into the marriage.

LOOKING IN THE MIRROR

Probably a day doesn't go by that we don't look in the mirror. Usually we spend several minutes or more in the mirror. We examine our hair, face, shave, clothes, etc. We wouldn't dare leave the mirror until everything was just right. When we look in the mirror, we are looking to see that things are proper.

The natural mirror is ideal for checking the outer appearance and beauty. But what's really important is, "How do we check to see if our heart is right?"

In The Book of James, Chapter 1:23,24 (NIV), the Word tells us, ***"Anyone who listens to the word but does not do what it says is like a man who looks at his face in a mirror and after looking at himself, goes away and immediately forgets what he looks like."*** If you want to know what your heart looks like or if you want to know what is in your heart, the Word of God is that mirror. Among other more important things, the Word will tell you if your heart is right toward your wife. Do you love her as God instructs you to? Do you love her regardless? Do you love and take care of her as you do yourself?

The Word will also tell you if you have hurt, pain, anger, bitterness, jealousy, lust, etc., in your heart. If God's mirror is revealing some things that are not in line with His Word, don't just try to walk away and forget it; fix it. ***"But the man who looks intently into the perfect law that gives freedom, and continues to do this, not forgetting what he has heard, but doing it – he will be blessed in what he does (verse 25)."***

Be a doer and not just a hearer of the Word…and you will be blessed in what you do.

Bless you wife by looking into God's mirror and taking action when necessary.

LOOKING IN THE MIRROR (II)

You can find a mirror that will let you see exactly what you want to see. If you want to see yourself as slender, there is a mirror for you. If you want to see yourself fat, there is a mirror for you. If you want to see yourself as Okay, there is a mirror for you. Just about any way you want to see yourself, that pleases you, there is a mirror for you. There are mirrors out there that will tell you that you are cool, handsome, sexy, and irresistible. There are also mirrors that will tell you that pre-marital sex, infidelity, and divorce are acceptable. The problem is that these mirrors lie. Know that there is a mirror that will not, cannot, never has, and never will lie. That mirror is God's Word. God's mirror will tell you the truth, whether you want to see it, hear it, or not. This same mirror, the Word, has life changing power. ***"For the word of God is living and active. Sharper than any double-edged sword, it penetrates even to dividing soul and spirit, joints and marrow; it judges the thoughts and attitudes of the heart. Nothing in all creation is hidden from God's sight. Everything is uncovered and laid bare before the eyes of him to whom we must give account. (Hebrews 4:12,13 NIV)."*** Are you curious about your thoughts and attitude? Do you want to know if the love you have for your wife meets God's standard? Check out God's mirror; His mirror (His Word) will tell you the truth.

Know what God expects of you as a husband.

Bless her by knowing and living God's standard as a husband toward his wife.

A LOVING HUSBAND...

As married couples we are to honor Christ by submitting to one another. Specifically, wives are to submit to their husband's leadership in the same way they submit to the Lord. Husbands are given a specific duty, which is to love their wives. Husbands must even be willing to go as far as Christ did in His love for the Church. We have done a lot of talking about love but not about what love is. Until we really study what is actually involved, we may think that it is easier for the husband to love his wife than for the wife to submit to her husband's leadership. This is because a husband thinks that loving his wife is something he does anyway.

Marriages have problems at one point or another and most always seem to overcome. Those that overcome often attribute it to the fact that they really do love each other. There are certain characteristics of love that husbands should display. Part of the problem is that we don't always display these critical characteristics. These characteristics, traits, or marks are found in First Corinthians 13:4-8. Take a look. Are you displaying patience, kindness, endurance, faith, hope, etc., as a husband?

So over the next few lessons we will address these characteristics and you will have the opportunity to do a self-examination. No score is given, but you will know where you stand.

The characteristics of a loving husband
Scriptural Foundation

1 Corinthians 13:4-8a

King James Version

"Charity suffereth long, and is kind; charity envieth not; charity vaunteth not itself, is not puffed up, Doth not behave itself unseemly, seeketh not her own, is not easily provoked, thinketh no evil; rejoiceth not in iniquity, but rejoiceth in the truth; beareth all things, believeth all things, hopeth all things, endureth all things, charity never faileth."

The Living Bible

Love is very patient and kind, never jealous or envious, never boastful or proud, never haughty or selfish or rude. Love does not demand its own way. It is not irritable or touchy. It does not hold grudges and will hardly even notice when others do it wrong. It is never glad about injustice, but rejoices whenever truth wins out. If you love someone you will be loyal to him no matter what the cost. You will always believe in him, always expect the best of him, and always stand your ground in defending him. All the special gifts and powers from God will someday come to an end, but love goes on forever.

The Amplified Bible

Love endures long and is patient and kind; love never is envious nor boils over with jealousy, is not boastful or vainglorious, does not display itself haughtily. It is not conceited (arrogant and inflated with pride); it is not rude (unmannerly) and does not act unbecomingly. Love (God's love in us) does not insist on its own rights or its own way, for it is not self-seeking; it is not touchy or fretful; it takes no account of the evil done to it [it pays no attention to a suffered wrong]. It does not rejoice at injustice and unrighteousness, but rejoices when right and truth prevail. Love bears up under anything and everything that comes, is ever ready to believe the best of every person, its hopes are fadeless under all circumstances, and it endures everything [without weakening]. Love never fails [never fades out or becomes obsolete or comes to an end].

The New International Version

Love is patient, love is kind. It does not envy, it does not boast, it is not proud. It is not rude, it is not self-seeking, it is not easily angered, it keeps no record of wrongs. Love does not delight in evil but rejoices with the truth. It always protects, always trusts, always hopes, always perseveres. Love never fails.

The Husbands, Love Your Wives... Version

A loving husband is a Godly husband. A loving husband is of God; therefore, he is patient, kind, not envious, does not boast and is not proud. He is not rude, self-seeking, easily angered, and he keeps no record of wrongs. A Godly husband is love, and he does not delight in evil but rejoices with the truth. He always protects, always trusts, always hopes, always perseveres. A Godly husband never fails his wife because he is love, and he loves her as Christ loves the church.

A LOVING HUSBAND IS PATIENT

A loving husband is patient, endures, and suffers long. Perhaps there is a situation that you have been praying about, but God seems to be moving slowly to answer your prayers. It may be an unsaved loved one or it may even be your wife. Are you willing to wait patiently on the Lord? Are you willing to stay and continue to pray so that God can work through you? Are you willing to endure the pain and suffering that you may be experiencing so that God's will can be done? While you are being patient, how's your composure and attitude? Can you still smile? Can you still rejoice? Consider the patience and suffering Christ endured and is enduring for us. There is really no comparison when you think of His death on the cross to pay the penalty for our sins.

A LOVING HUSBAND IS KIND

A loving husband is kind. There will be times when your wife will need a sympathetic shoulder to lean or cry on. Are you available to be sympathetic towards her or are you too hard and too "macho?" A loving husband knows how to be his wife's best friend, how to be there for her when she needs him. He knows how to comfort and encourage her in difficult times. Is your wife afraid to talk with you about her concerns or needs? Does she often have to go to a girlfriend or even worst, "a boyfriend?" A loving husband knows how to be gentle and generous to his wife. Are you always taking instead of giving? There are a lot of expensive gifts out there for you to buy and give to your wife, but the best gift is free. Give her what she needs – a loving and devoted husband.

A LOVING HUSBAND IS NOT ENVIOUS

A loving husband is not envious or jealous. There is no place for envy within a marriage. Since the two of you are "one," it would be like the hands envying the head because the head seems more important. If it weren't for the hands, the head would have to eat from a plate the same way a dog eats. Be content when your partner succeeds. Her success is your success, and your success is her success. If she does something that causes you to be jealous of other men, communicate your thoughts and perceptions to her in a kind and gentle way. Loyalty and devotion to one another eliminates the resentfulness and rage that can result from jealousy. Jealousy as in being watchful, careful, and protective of her innocence in a cruel and vicious world is necessary. Never attempt to intentionally make your wife jealous. A lot of times you can do it unintentionally. Making the partner jealous is like when we were kids. As kids, we would play-fight and this would often progress to an actual fight or someone getting hurt. Your attempt to make her jealous may cause her to go out and do what she perceives that you are doing.

A LOVING HUSBAND IS NEVER BOASTFUL

A loving husband is never boastful or proud. Being boastful is when pride and satisfaction are out of control. It is an overrated opinion of oneself and exaggerated self-esteem. Are you successful because of what you did or are you successful as a direct result of God's blessings and divine favor? The Bible has many warnings about pride, boasting, and thinking of oneself more highly than we ought. The same way boasting turns away friends and God, it also can also turn away your wife. We are encouraged to give all thanks, all glory, all praise, and all honor to God for it is He who gives us the power and ability to get wealth and succeed. When you have a need to boast, boast in the Lord.

A LOVING HUSBAND IS NOT HAUGHTY

A loving husband does not behave unseemly or haughty. Similar to being boastful and proud, unseemly and haughty actions are not proper either. Also, while showing great pride in oneself, one shows contempt and scorn for others. You know, the inflated puffed-up ego, the nose in the air, the head too big to fit through the door. This includes being just plain rude and disrespectful. In your opinion, "Are you more important than others?" Do you have to be the loudest in the conversation? In your attempt to be seen or noticed, do you often offend others?

A LOVING HUSBAND IS NOT DEMANDING

A loving husband does not seek his own or demand his own way. A good example is, "It's either my way, or you can hit the highway" or "It's my way, or no way." It pays to discuss things with your wife. She is your partner. God gave her to you to help you and to make you complete. Not discussing things with her would be like having a wealth of knowledge and experience and not using it. If you have a business partner, you might not be in business together very long if you don't discuss things before making decisions. A husband should not use physical or other abusive means to force his wife to do things his way. Rather, he should treat his wife with respect, as the physically weaker partner. Consider putting her needs before your own.

A LOVING HUSBAND IS NOT EASILY PROVOKED

A loving husband is not easily provoked or is not irritable or touchy. Do minor things that go wrong send you into a rage? Does the traffic on the way home have you so irritable that you unload on the first person you see? Do you perceive every comment made to you as a personal attack? Is the family afraid to meet you at the door when you come home because they are not sure what kind of mood you will be in? Could your personality be characterized as Dr. Jeckel and Mr. Hyde? When you get angry, do you turn a different color? When the Hulk got angry, he turned green. The Hulk had an anger problem for which he was constantly seeking a cure. In real-life there is a cure, it's called deliverance.

A LOVING HUSBAND IS NOT GRUDGED

A loving husband does not think evil nor does he hold grudges. Thinking evil includes thinking about another woman in a sensual way, thinking of a way to get even, or thinking of a way to hurt or embarrass someone. A husband, with God's love, looks for the opportunity to get things right with his wife. He is quick to ask for and grant forgiveness or to say, "I'm sorry." When your wife or someone else does you wrong, are you thinking of evil ways to get even? A positive trait is that you may hardly even notice when others do you wrong. Holding grudges keeps you and the other person prisoner. We hold grudges to hurt the other person, but actually all parties concerned are hurt. The one holding the grudge has anger in their heart, which if not dealt with will turn into bitterness. In other words, holding a grudge is keeping record of how many times she has wronged you, even after you have forgiven her. Are there people you absolutely, positively refuse to speak to or have anything to do with? Is there an event in your past in which you have not truly forgiven someone? If so, get it right today. Set them and yourself free.

A LOVING HUSBAND IS NEVER GLAD ABOUT INJUSTICE

A loving husband does not rejoice in iniquity or is never glad about injustice. He never stands-in-wait for the opportunity to say, "I told you so," or "I knew they wouldn't make it." There are some sinful things going on in the world and especially on television. Most shows are depicting marriages tormented by extra-marital affairs, divorce, abuse, and murder to name a few. If you allow this type of programming to come into your home, you might as well be rejoicing in it. If there was not a demand for these types of programs (if people were not glad about the injustices), the television industry would have to change or go out of business.

A LOVING HUSBAND REJOICES IN TRUTH

A loving husband rejoices in the truth or rejoices whenever truth wins out. There will come a time when righteousness and truth will prevail. When we hear of or have the opportunity to participate in and celebrate a wedding anniversary, whether it is for one year or ten, we should be excited. Anytime a couple is blessed with another year of marriage together it calls for a celebration. God is pleased, so we should be totally thrilled. When couples renew their marital vows they are, in a sense, rejoicing, therefore we should rejoice with those who rejoice. When a Christian marriage endures the test of time and trials, it confirms to the world that God's Word is true and that accepting Christ is a life-changing event.

A LOVING HUSBAND BEARS ALL THINGS

A loving husband bears all things. When things get tough in the marriage, the husband (the head, the leader) should be the one to really dig in, believe God, stand on His Word, and not be moved. He should set an example for his wife and other couples looking at the relationship from the outside. Marriages will have problems, but only those who endure those things that come their way will survive. Your loyalty first goes to God, then to your wife. If you are loyal to God, you will be loyal to your wife. You can expect your loyalty to be tested each and every day. Be prepared. If you love her, you will be loyal no matter the cost. Loyalty also includes protecting her. Never talk bad about your wife or let anyone else talk bad about her. If anyone talks about her, they are also talking about you. Know that when you sin, you sin against God and the eyes of the Lord are in every place.

A LOVING HUSBAND BELIEVES IN HIS WIFE

A loving husband will always believe in his wife. You can always believe and trust in God. Also believe the best of your wife. By believing in her, she gains confidence and trust in you as someone who really cares about her and her needs. When she has a project or a special job to do, be the one to motivate and encourage her. Let her know that you are confident that she can do it. Remind her of the scripture that lets us know that we can do all things through Christ who gives us strength (Philippians 4:13). The husband should be the wife's biggest fan and cheerleader. He is always by her side reassuring her with the Word of God.

A LOVING HUSBAND HOPES ALL THINGS

A loving husband hopes all things. As a loving husband, you should always expect the best of your wife. Never fall for the temptation to give up on her and the marriage. That temptation doesn't come from God. God did not give up on us, so neither should we give up on our wives and marriages. Instead of God giving up on mankind, He always tried something or someone different. Last of all, He sent His Son. This is how we are to love our wives, ***"as Christ has loved the church and gave himself for it."*** Before God will tell you to give up, He will give you several other options. First, believe that God can and will do it. When things go haywire, expect God to restore the relationship.

A LOVING HUSBAND WILL ENDURE ALL THINGS

A loving husband will endure all things. Be willing to stand your ground in defending her. Realize that you are not only defending her, but you are defending yourself and what and whom you believe in. If you are willing and determined, love will cause you to endure the most difficult of times. Love will cause you to be willing to forgive or say that you are sorry. There will be so-called easy ways out of difficult situations, but take the one that God wants you to take. The law has provided several reasons for ending marriages, but what does God say?

A LOVING HUSBAND NEVER FAILS

A loving husband above all, never fails. There are a lot of things that are here today and gone tomorrow, but the love you have for your wife should never fade. If anything, you should get closer and your love should grow stronger. There are a lot of important and significant things in life, but your love for her takes top place (right under your love for God). God is love. God never fails. Love never fails. Because God is love, He has commanded us to love one another. This kind of love is a supernatural love. It's not lustful. God has poured out his love into our hearts by the Holy Spirit. When we first believed in Christ (accepted Him as Lord and Savior), the Holy Spirit filled our hearts with the love of God. Therefore, because our hearts are filled with the love of God, we are empowered to love the way God instructs us. We cannot love the way he wants us to without Him.

GOD CREATED SEX

Sex was God's idea and it was not created for the sole purpose of propagation (reproduction, breeding, multiplying). I refer back to Genesis 2:23-25 (NIV), ***"The man said, "This is now bone of my bones and flesh of my flesh; she shall be called 'woman,' for she was taken out of man." For this reason a man will leave his father and mother and be united to his wife, and they will become one flesh. The man and his wife were both naked, and they felt no shame."*** God set up marriage as a lifetime commitment and relationship. Sexual relations between the husband and wife consummate the marriage. When a husband makes love to his wife, it is a way that he shows his love and how he feels about her. Sex is a time for intimacy; it reaffirms oneness and commitment to one another. It is a time to re-unite. It shows a desire to submit to one another and fulfill each other's sexual needs. When a husband makes love to his wife, he should put her needs before his own. When God created, fashioned, and formed woman, He did so to make her suitable for man in every way (mentally, physically, spiritually, socially, emotionally, and yes sexually). Adam and Eve enjoyed sex in a clean and intimate way before the fall. Even today, it is sin that distorts God's intention for sex. It was God Himself who concluded that it was not good for Adam to be alone. Adam also came to the self-realization that he needed a suitable partner, friendship, and intimacy from a creature similar to himself. Therefore, the husband and wife need each other as a friend, a partner, and a lover. God created us with a sexual desire for the opposite sex, and He made it clear what makes it right -- that being within the context of marriage between one man and one women (in sickness and in health, for richer or for poorer, until death do you apart).

Besides propagation, sex promotes love and communication between the husband and wife. Sex between the husband and wife also prevents (deters) the desire to fornicate (the unlawful, unrighteous satisfaction of a God-given sexual desire).

Bless her by clearing up the myth and thought that sex (within your marriage) is bad, evil, or unimportant.

UNQUESTIONABLE FREEDOM

Another hindrance to truly being ***"one"*** in marriage is the past. In most cases, before and after marriage, we did not conduct our lives as God had intended. This brings unnecessary baggage into the marriage. Whether we were ignorant to His Word or not, we often fell short of what God expected (saved or unsaved). Even when forgiven, oftentimes the enemy will bring up our past in an attempt to hinder our walk with God and our relationship with our wives. The enemy is counting on us to forget or not trust God's Word (promises) to us. God's Word confirms His forgiveness towards us when we fall short (sin). Those you hurt may forgive you, giving you a sense of freedom, but true and unquestionable freedom comes from Jesus. Jesus himself said as recorded in John 8:36, ***"Therefore if the Son makes you free, you shall be free indeed."*** Sin confessed to God is instantly and eternally forgiven. Unquestionable freedom gives you the ability to be all that God intended – a husband and wife who are one, a husband who loves his wife as Christ loves the church, a wife who yields to her husband's leadership and respects him. Remember that you can't change the past, but unquestionable freedom means there is no need to carry the guilt of past failures and forgiven sins.

Jesus grants us relief from the "excess baggage" of life. In return, He gives us unquestionable freedom to be the strong, spiritual husband He intends.

Bless her by being free indeed!

UNQUESTIONABLE FREEDOM (II)

Did your marriage get off to a bad start? Were there times of inconsistency? Are you feeling guilty of wrongs? Are you feeling condemned? Are you feeling hopeless? Are you being beat up by your past? If you are, my advice is simply "Get in!" "Yes, Get in Christ Jesus!" ***"There is therefore now no condemnation to those who are <u>in Christ Jesus</u>, who do not walk according to the flesh, but according to the Spirit (Romans 8:1 NKJV)."*** So again I say, "Get in Christ Jesus!" Now if you are "In Christ Jesus," and you are still feeling guilt from the past, condemnation, and hopelessness, I would encourage you to check your walk. Are you a Christian, but your walk is controlled by the flesh? It is one thing to be in Christ, it's another thing to be controlled and guided by the Holy Spirit. No matter how bad a marriage may seem, if it is in Christ, it is not condemned. There is hope. The husband and wife simply need to check their walk. Sin brings bondage, but confession and forgiveness bring unquestionable freedom. God has promised us that, ***"If we confess our sins, he [God] is faithful and just to forgive us our sins, and to cleanse us from all unrighteousness (1 John 1:9 KJV)."*** God has assured us that He will do his part to forgive, we just have to do our part to confess.

Our marriages should be free from regrets of the past. We have all made mistakes, but God has given us a way to flow in unquestionable freedom.

Bless her by letting your walk be controlled by the Holy Spirit.

HONOR MARRIAGE

We live in a time where, in most cases, marriage is anything but honored. Governments, courts, and even some marriage counselors have low regard for marriage as God intended. Marriage is a divine, sacred institution designed by God to form a permanent union and bond between a man and a woman. Marriage joins a man and woman as husband and wife (becoming one flesh). Our scripture, Hebrews 13:4a (NIV), states that, ***"Marriage should be honored by all."*** Since we live in a society that does not hold marriage in high regard or great respect, we should take every opportunity to do what the Word of God tells us. It starts with each of us. As husbands and wives, have a good reputation and demonstrate a marriage under God's control. Fight against those things that attempt to dishonor your marriage, anyone else's, or marriage as an institution of God. Settle for nothing less. It's important to celebrate your anniversary and renew your wedding vows; that's all a part of honoring marriage. When another couple celebrates their anniversary, celebrate with them. Let them know that you treasure their marriage; rejoice with them that rejoice and weep with them that weep. Another part of honoring marriage is to not let anyone or anything come between you and your wife.

Do your part to honor marriage every chance you get.

Bless her by holding your marriage in high regards, showing her just how important marriage is to you.

HONOR MARRIAGE (II)

In a society that disregards and disrespects marriage, here are a few helpful solutions for various situations.

- When you think divorce is the answer,
honor marriage.
- When you want to separate,
honor marriage.
- When you think of another woman,
honor marriage.
- When you feel like giving up,
honor marriage.
- When you feel like fighting,
honor marriage.
- When you want to retaliate with mean words,
honor marriage.
- When you want to get even,
honor marriage.
- When lustful thoughts come,
honor marriage.
- When no one else cares,
honor marriage.
- When no one else is looking,
honor marriage
- When you are hurting,
honor marriage.
- When away on business,
honor Marriage.
- When the co-worker flirts,
honor marriage.

"Marriage should be honored by all. (Hebrews 13:4a NIV)." Therefore, honor God by honoring marriage.

You can indirectly honor God by directly honoring marriage.

Bless her by honoring her, your marriage, and God in every situation.

HONOR MARRIAGE (III)

Understand that marriage, and marriage as an institution, honors God. But amongst each other, we have a decision to make each and every day regarding marriage. We must make a choice and that choice is manifested through our actions, whether we (as husbands and wives) honor marriage. Hebrews 13:4a, The Amplified Bible states, ***"Let marriage be held in honor (esteemed worthy, precious, of great price and especially dear) in all things."*** The word "Let" implies that the honor of marriage does not just happen; some action on our part is required. We have to make, allow, or permit the honor of marriage. While doing so, we must also support marriage and keep the honor from falling. Honoring marriage has to be an active, unbroken, and unyielding part of our daily lives.

God instituted marriage as a precious, pure, sacred, and permanent union of a man and woman. Therefore, it is safe to say and assume that the devil, our enemy, is against marriage. Satan is working to dishonor and defile marriage; so with God's help (favor), we need to do our part to keep marriage held in high regards. ***"He who finds a wife finds a good thing, and obtains favor from the Lord."*** Proverbs 18:22 (NKJV) has assured us that when it comes to marriage (as He intended), God is on our side.

Recognize that there is an enemy working against marriages, but more importantly, realize that The True and Living God Almighty is here and ready to bestow favor in our marriages.

Bless her by letting the honor of your marriage be manifested daily.

A GOOD THING

Almost any man can find a woman to be his wife. But, ***"He who finds a [true] wife finds a good thing and obtains favor from the Lord (Proverbs 18-22 AMP)."*** A man who marries a capable, intelligent, and virtuous woman has truly found a good thing. She is described as being far more precious and valuable than jewels, rubies, pearls, etc. (Proverbs 31:10 AMP). But what could make anyone so precious and valuable? Is it the outer beauty, such as hair, nails, figure, complexion, walk, or clothes? Is it how one can lay on the charm through attractiveness and fascination? The secret (which is really not a secret) that makes her a "good (precious and valuable) thing" is her relationship with God and empowerment by Holy Spirit. To her faith she adds virtue, to her virtue she adds knowledge, to her knowledge she adds self-control, to her self-control she adds perseverance, to her perseverance she adds godliness, to godliness she adds brotherly kindness, and to brotherly kindness she adds love. When these are hers and are plentiful she will neither be barren or unfruitful in the knowledge of her Lord and Savior, Jesus Christ (paraphrased from 2 Peter 1:5-8). ***"Charm can be deceptive and beauty doesn't last, but a woman who fears and reverences God shall be greatly praised (Proverbs 31:30 TLB)."***

Husbands – The reverent and worshipful fear of the Lord is the true and solid foundation that makes the marriage obtain God's favor.

Wives – The reverent and worshipful fear of the Lord is the true and solid foundation that makes your value "far above rubies or pearls."

In a more important aspect, Jesus Christ and His gift of salvation is truly a good thing.

Bless her by ensuring that your marriage has a true and solid foundation.

MARRIAGE NEEDS FRIENDSHIP

When it comes to friendship, there is no better friend than that of Jesus Christ. He's a friend who sticks closer than a brother. He's a friend who will never fail. He will always be there. He's never too busy. He always has the answer, and He will never pretend to be your friend. Your marriage has a friend. "What a friend we have in Jesus." Besides Jesus, your wife needs you as her next best friend. When the two of you work together toward the same goals (as opposed to working toward different goals) the accomplishments and benefits are obvious. Because you work together and are so close, when one is down physically, emotionally, or spiritually the other should be right there to pull them up and encourage them. It's a cold night even in the middle of summer when she has to sleep without you. There can also be cold nights although the two of you are in bed together. Many marriages have endured and will continue to endure because the husband and wife stood back-to-back defending their relationship against the enemy. When one was down, the other was providing comfort, ministering to the need, and standing guard with prayer. Finally, with Jesus as the tie that binds the husband and wife together, the marriage can endure, even in the most difficult situations. Please see Proverbs 18:24 and Ecclesiastes 4:9-12 (Two are better than one… A cord of three strands is not quickly broken).

Remember that friends know each other well, they are close acquaintances, they are supportive of each other, and on the same side in a struggle (never hostile toward each other). A marriage without friendship is missing a key ingredient.

Bless her by being her next best friend first, her husband second, and her lover third.

AT ALL TIMES

"A friend loveth at all times… (Proverbs 17:17a KJV)." At all times? Yes, at all times. Sounds like a tall order to fill, and it is. There is only one perfect friend, and that's Jesus. So as husbands, we are the next best friends because we are not perfect. However, we must be the best friends that we can be. We all have faults, so periodically our friendship toward our wives may fail. If we want to be a husband (friend) who loves his wife at all times, we will need help. We will need the love of God as described in I Corinthians 13. We need love that is patient and kind, while not being envious, boastful, proud, rude, self-seeking, and easily angered. This love does not keep record of wrongs and does not delight in evil; rather it rejoices with the truth, protects, trusts, hopes, and perseveres. Finally, this love never fails. This is how a husband (friend) can love at all times. In Romans 5:5, Paul the writer lets us know that, "…God has poured out His love into our hearts by the Holy Spirit, whom he has given us." So even in the midst of whatever comes up against your marriage, you'll have the love to keep on loving. Love is a fruit of the Spirit. Love is evidence that the Holy Spirit is in control of your life. It is this kind of love that exercises authority in a difficult situation and will not allow you to "blow your lid" or give her "a piece of your mind." This love does not tolerate sin or sinful behavior; rather it is willing to tell the hard truth.

What kind of friend are you to your wife? Yes, loving (your wife) at all times may be difficult (Equally as difficult is a wife loving her husband at all times). As hard as you may try on your own, you will need help and that help is available through an intimate and personal relationship with God through His Son Jesus Christ.

Bless her by showing her that, "with God, nothing shall be impossible," even being a husband and friend that loves her – at all times.

IT'S IN THERE

First Samuel 16:7, in part says ***"Man looks at the outward appearance, but the Lord looks at the heart."*** God so uniquely fashioned woman that Adam couldn't help but proclaim, ***"This is now bone of my bones, and flesh of my flesh: she shall be called Woman, because she was taken out of Man (Genesis 2:23 KJV)."*** Adam viewed Eve as God viewed Eve. Adam realized that everything he needed from an earthly companion was standing right there in front of him. He realized that he needed her to be complete himself. Although Adam did not know of a father and mother as we do, God said, ***"For this reason a man will leave his father and mother and be united to his wife, and they will become one flesh (Genesis 2:24 NIV)."*** The bond of marriage is so powerful because that is what God intended. Besides God, everything you need, from relationship to just plain companionship, is in her. When one starts viewing his wife as God views her, he will realize that God awesomely fashioned her for a divine purpose in his life. Look beyond the face, the hair, and the curves, and check out her inner beauty. The two of you together bring out the best in each other. There are undiscovered treasures in your wife, the wife that you greet in the morning, kiss good bye, hold tightly at night, and sometimes take for granted. Search deeply – "It's in there,"

Stop worrying about what you think other husbands have; rather, focus on what God has given you and focus on that which is yet to be discovered within her.

Bless her by placing emphasis on the fact that she is exactly what you need and nothing less. God has never done an incomplete work. In everything He has a divine purpose.

NO SHAME

Genesis 2:25 (NIV), "The man and his wife were both naked, and they felt no shame." Physically, they were wearing no clothes. Physically, we often get naked. But what was so important with Adam and Eve is that they were not hiding anything from each other. At this point they were completely open to each other. There was no deceit, no pride, no envy, no strife, no bitterness, and no jealousy. There was no reason to hide anything. They truly understood what it meant to "be one." Everything was beautiful; there was no fear, no guilt, and no sin.

Secrets and hidden agendas in marriage bring fear, guilt, and resentment. Imagine the comfort and peace when you are alone showering or getting dressed; there is no fear or shame. But fear sets in the moment there is a threat of someone violating your privacy. Get naked and stay naked as in truly honest and open with your wife. When there is nothing to hide there is complete freedom to be yourself. Sin distorts the relationship between the husband and wife. The sin may not be adultery or fornication. It may just be a lack of faith in God, a lack of believing that He is who He says He is, a lack of believing that He can heal the relationship, or a lack of believing in His Son, Jesus.

When we realize and accept the fact that we are naked in the sight of God, and that absolutely nothing is hid from Him, that begins our intimate relationship with Him.

Bless her by getting naked with her, beyond just taking off your clothes.

FLESH OF MY FLESH

Although Adam had conversations with God and even named the animals, none of the actual words of those conversations were recorded. Now God had done miraculous things before Adam's very eyes. The Lord had planted the Garden of Eden and placed Adam there to take care of it. He gave him a job. The Lord gave him the "Do's and Do nots" of the Garden. Then the Lord began forming animals from the ground and gave Adam the privilege to name them. Adam witnessed and was a part of it all. But for God's next creation, He caused Adam to go into a deep sleep. It's important to note that of all that had been accomplished in Adam's presence, the very first words of his, recorded in the Bible (Genesis 2:23 NIV) were his comments about his wife. ***"This is now bone of my bones and flesh of my flesh; she shall be called 'woman,' for she was taken out of man."*** In a sense, he was saying, God, of all the miraculous things You have done, 'This is it!' The trees, the Garden, the plants, and the animals are nice, but she is it! She is someone I can relate to. She is a part of my very own bone and flesh. She is what I have been missing.

When we view wives as "bone of our bones and flesh of our flesh," the marriage takes on new meaning. She's not just a woman or just a wife; she is a part of the husband.

My wife is bone of my bones and flesh of my flesh and I am excited about it! How about you and yours?

DIVINE FAVOR

"Whoso findeth a wife findeth a good thing, and obtaineth favour of the Lord" (Proverbs 18:22 KJV). There will come a time in marriage when your money, your job, your status, and even your friends will not be able to help. There are some things money (or credit cards) can't buy. There are some things that the most satisfying jobs can't do for you. There are some things your status has no influence over. Sometimes a friend can only be there for support. When trouble comes in the marriage, it has no regard for how much money you have, who you work for, or whether you are the boss or the janitor. It has no regard for whether you are best friends with the President or have no friends at all. What's important to know is that there is Divine favor available during the good and bad times in a marriage. Within the marriage, you should know one thing, that God has obligated Himself to show Divine favor in your marriage. Wealth or worldly status does not obtain this favor; rather, it is a Divine gift of God. There is no reward for just being married, but marriage is an institute of God. It shows that you have chosen God's way as opposed to the world's way of cohabitation. Anytime you choose God's way over the world's way, you can expect "Divine favor."

God's divine favor will do what no one or no thing can do for your marriage. It's mightier than money, it goes beyond your status, it comes through like no friend can – it's precious, it's supernatural, and it's God!

Bless her by letting showers of God's Divine favor protect, refresh, and rejuvenate your marriage. Let God do for your marriage what no one else can.

DON'T BE HARSH

Before you act, think about how you would like to be treated. Nobody normally wants to be mistreated or hurt. As a rule for the Christian home, the Amplified Bible says in ***Colossians 3:19 (AMP), "Husbands, love your wives [be affectionate, and sympathetic with them] and do not be harsh or bitter or resentful toward them."*** Affection is an important need of a wife. Unfortunately, it seems easier for a husband to be harsh than to be affectionate. Work at being affectionate to your wife. If the marriage is struggling and there seems to be distance between the two of you, know that this is not the way God wants the relationship. Affection starts by showing her that she is special to you. A simple hug, kiss, or gentle touch can say more than the famous words "I love you." Some husbands haven't even grasped the concept of telling their wives that they love them. Often they assume that the wives know it already. God encourages us to take it a step further, not to just love each other in words alone, but in our actions and in truth. Being harsh and bitter will cause a marriage to grow cold. If a marriage has grown cold, practicing sincere affection will light the fire in a marriage and help keep it lit.

BLESS HER

What's so important about blessing your wife? Usually, being a blessing is about meeting a need. A wife's needs go beyond those basic necessities, such as food, clothing, shelter, physical security, etc. One of the important things about a husband blessing his wife is that he is meeting her inner needs. Unfortunately, there are times when the marriage relationship is disintegrating from the inside out. The physical needs are met and the emotional needs are left unfulfilled. The wife is aware that her needs are not being met and the husband thinks everything is okay. In Ephesians 5, Jesus gives us his example of what the marriage relationship should be like. Specifically, in Ephesians 5:25-27 the scripture shows how Christ meets the needs of His Church. It is in this same way that a husband should meet the needs of his wife. Most importantly, it is God who equips the husband to identify and meet the needs of his wife.

It's amazing what even a small blessing can do in a marriage. Just as a wife can use a blessing, so can the husband. One blessing will generate another blessing in return. Allow God to use you as an instrument or vessel to channel blessings to your wife. When you bless her, it will give her an uncontrollable desire to be a blessing to you.

A PART OF ME

Ephesians 5:28 (TLB), "That is how husbands should treat their wives, loving them as parts of themselves. For since a man and his wife are now one, a man is really doing himself a favor and loving himself when he loves his wife!" As a husband and wife celebrate their anniversary, it allows them the opportunity to reflect on how much fun they have together and how much they appreciate each other. The closer a couple is to truly being one, the easier it is to have fun and really enjoy each other. Realize that your wife is not just your wife, she is actually a part of you. Loving and caring for your wife is actually loving and caring for yourself. A man who loves his wife loves himself.

"His and Hers" items (such as towels and cars) can be nice, but don't let them work against the idea and goal of being one. "That's my car!" "That's my money!" "That's her job!" Phrases such as these can and do hinder God's idea and plan for husbands and wives to be one. There is nothing hidden when a husband and wife are one, and they are working toward the same goal. Remember, "oneness" between husband and wife is God's idea.

WHO'S BUILDING THE HOUSE?

Psalm 127:1a (NIV), "Unless the Lord builds the house, its builders labor in vain." We are not necessarily talking about a house. It could very easily be prosperity, prestige, a sense of security, or even a relationship. The real question is "Who's building your marriage?" Is your marriage built by your power and your might? Marriage is an institution of God. He created marriage. He knows how it should work. He knows how to help you build a closer relationship, and when a marriage is broken or has problems, He knows how to fix them. Even the first marriage between Adam and Eve had its problems. You can be sure that if their marriage had problems, yours will also. Knowing that troubles will come, it is important to know that we need God to help us make this thing called "marriage" work. Our marriages are what they are "by the grace of God." His word says it rains on the just and the unjust. So you will see successful non-Christian marriages, but real prosperity, prestige, and security comes from a personal and intimate relationship with God. God's Word, The Holy Bible, is like medicine to a marriage. It will do no good sitting on the counter or coffee table; it must be taken in your heart and applied in your life. Just as you would tell your child to open his or her mouth for a spoonful of life saving medicine, I'm telling you to open your heart for a dose of God's marriage saving Word.

MISSING ELEMENTS

(Part I)

"Likewise, ye husbands, dwell with them according to knowledge, giving honour unto the wife, as unto the weaker vessel, and as being heirs together of the grace of life; that your prayers be not hindered (1 Peter 3:7 KJV)."

Most marriages that end, don't just "crash and burn," rather they simply die a slow death. It's sort of like a disease as opposed to a heart attack, like when husbands and wives stop living together according to what they know is right. Wives have their duty in the marriage and husbands do also. Often husbands know exactly how to treat their wives, but fail to do it. Husbands often know how to meet their needs, but fail to do it. Sometimes pride, the ego, and bitterness get in the way. A wife needs compassion, understanding, and consideration from her husband. Consideration of her feelings used to be the first thought, now the thought seldom comes to mind. What are her needs? Does she need someone to talk to? Be there for her. Listen to her. The same tenderness and affection that was there in the early months and years of marriage are still needed. The thoughtfulness of flowers, time together, and getaways are still needed. Don't let the thoughtfulness slowly disappear. Don't let compassion, understanding, and consideration become "missing elements."

MISSING ELEMENTS
(Part II)

"Likewise, ye husbands, dwell with them according to knowledge, giving honour unto the wife, as unto the weaker vessel, and as being heirs together of the grace of life; that your prayers be not hindered (1 Peter 3:7 KJV)."

This scripture also helps us to realize once again that a husband and his wife are "one." They are in this gift called "life" together. How one treats his wife, directly affects his relationship with the Lord. There are three points to remember that lead up to one major point:

1. Be considerate of her and of the marital relationship. Don't do things that put the marriage in jeopardy.

2. Honor and respect her as being the physically weaker partner. Although she may be physically capable, honor and protect her by doing those things that are physically demanding. Allow her to save her energy for other things.

3. Together, there are blessings of unmerited favor in store. Know that God wants to bless your marriage.

Whether you view the scripture as referring to physical differences or God's pattern for the home, when things are not right in the marriage, it puts a strain on other areas of your life. When communication between a husband and wife become weak or poor it can affect a husband's prayers to God. This can be dangerous because a husband needs his guidance and instructions from God. Do what is right in God's sight within the marriage. A husband and wife working and praying together can accomplish so much more. There is a lot to be done in a marriage. She has special talent and abilities and so does the husband. A husband and wife need each other. Don't let communication and conversation become missing elements.

MISSING ELEMENTS

(Part III)

"Husbands, likewise, dwell with them [wives] with understanding, giving honor to the wife, as to the weaker vessel, and as being heirs together of the grace of life, that your prayers may not be hindered (I Peter 3:7 NKJV)."

God instructs the husband to "give honor to the wife." Yes, all honor belongs to God. In honoring (showing great regard and respect to) your wife you are honoring marriage and honoring God. You are being obedient to God's Word. Anytime you are obedient to God's Word (in love), you honor God. When husbands honor their wives they are carrying out God's plan for the marriage. Honor is an essential (and sometimes missing) element of the godly marriage. In fact, she deserves great honor. I know a man who has a clear understanding and a strong grasp of what God is telling husbands in this scripture. When introducing his wife to others, he always refers to her as his "Queen." That taught me a lot about honoring my wife. In the natural, a queen is the wife of a king. No one addresses the queen or king without first giving them honor. When a husband refers to his wife as queen, he places himself in the position as king. The king and queen have need of each other. We honor each other so that there be no division in the marriage (I Corinthians 12:23-25).

MISSING ELEMENTS
(Part IV)

"Husbands, likewise, dwell with them [wives] with understanding, giving honor to the wife, as to the weaker vessel, and as being heirs together of the grace of life, that your prayers may not be hindered (I Peter 3:7 NKJV)."

Many of us may have wives capable of doing many things that are physically demanding. There are some wives who can single-handedly move couches, dressers, and refrigerators. They are even capable taking out the trash and closing their own car door. The husband of the marriage should strive to handle the physically demanding tasks, if he does not have a physical disability. This type of honor to the wife shows her that you care about her well being. It also prevents her from having rougher hand than you have. Physically, God created the man stronger, yet equal to his wife. God gave you a helper, suitable to your needs, not a maid. She is a helper that God intended to be what the man cannot. You are also a helper intended to be and do what the wife cannot.

Neither the husband nor the wife should have to fend for themselves. Be thoughtful of her needs. Make sure she knows she is important to you. She may be physically able to do everything you can do, and may be able to do it better, but let her exert her energy in other ways (as God intended) to be a blessing to you, the marriage, and the family. By ensuring she gets proper rest, you may be surprised at the energy she has to honor and pamper you. Don't let chivalry (courage, honor, and a readiness to help the weak and protect women) become a missing element in your marriage.

MISSING ELEMENTS
(Part V)

"Husbands, likewise, dwell with them [wives] with understanding, giving honor to the wife, as to the weaker vessel, and as being heirs together of the grace of life, that your prayers may not be hindered (I Peter 3:7 NKJV)."

Marriage is your greatest investment. It is not necessarily the job, the degree, or the business. Some may say their house, their car, their stocks, etc. Because marriage is such a great investment, it requires work and a lot of attention. I have come to appreciate the fact that my wife and I are heirs together of the grace of life, "partners in receiving God's blessings." I also have come to realize that jobs, houses, and cars come and go. There will come a time when the job is over and the wife is still there. There will come a time when one will move from one house to another but the wife is still there. Cars are changed out frequently, but the wife is still there. If we live long enough and the Lord delays His Second Coming, we will eventually retire and those material things that may have been important then may not be as important upon retirement.

In all that we do on a daily basis, make a solid, consistent, and lasting investment in your wife and the marriage. There is no greater, more satisfying "partnership" than that of a husband and wife. This "partnership," when executed as God intended, will set you up for God's blessings and unmerited favor. God pours into the marriage where the husband and wife pour into each other. Don't let the "partnership" become a missing element in your marriage.

MISSING ELEMENTS
(Part VI)

"Husbands, likewise, dwell with them [wives] with understanding, giving honor to the wife, as to the weaker vessel, and as being heirs together of the grace of life, that your prayers may not be hindered (I Peter 3:7 NKJV)."

There are enough things the enemy throws at us to hinder our prayers, so don't let the way we treat our wives and our marriages be one of them. This scripture puts in perspective how God views marriage, the husband and wife relationship. If there are missing elements in the marriage, such as lack of communication between husband and wife; careful consideration of the wife; thoughtfulness of her needs; honor to the wife; an intelligent recognition of the marriage relationship; and joint partnership, then your relationship with God can be affected. Have you ever had a disagreement or argument with your wife and the communication went to zero? Then when you get to church or work you try to talk and carry on as if all is well? The hindrance comes from having bitterness or unforgiveness toward your wife while trying to have an intimate conversation with God, asking God to forgive you while you are not forgiving her.

On the other hand, get ready for effective, answered prayers when there are no missing elements and those listed above are in full force in your marriage. God wants to hear from and bless those who are doing things His way. Trust that God will never guide you the wrong way. God says that by trusting Him with all your heart, not leaning to your own understanding, and by always acknowledging Him, He will direct your paths (Proverbs 3:5-6). This includes marriage.

IN NEED OF LIFTING

"Pleasant words are as an honeycomb, sweet to the soul, and health to the bone (Proverbs 16:24 KJV)." Is she in need of lifting? There are times when she may feel discouraged or a lack of encouragement; things are not okay. It is amazing what a kind word can do. Kind words can take her and your marriage to the next level. You have the power (through carefully chosen words) to touch her very soul. Your words can be enjoyable and healthful. Think about some of the words you have used recently towards your wife. Were they pleasant, kind, encouraging, and sweet? Did they speak life, health, and prosperity into the situation? Just as honey can be used as a natural sweetener for various foods, pleasant words can be used as a means to reach parts of her that you can't touch any other way. When she is bitter, send a sweetener. When she is broken hearted, send healing directly to where it hurts. When her heart simply aches, send soothing medicine. Through God's Word, you can minister healing that no medicine can even come close to doing. When she needs lifting, it's from the inside. Pleasant words begin in your heart, are thought out in your mind, and are verbalized with your mouth. Pleasant words must be spoken to be effective.

MORE LIKE HIM

"Husbands, love your wives, just as Christ also loved the church and gave Himself for it, … (Ephesians 5:25 NKJV)." Not like husbands in the world, but like husbands who are in Christ. In our relationship with our wives, let's strive to have a marital relationship more like Christ towards the church. Don't necessarily wait for the wife to show love and kindness, be the one to initiate and sustain the wonderful relationship that should exist in a marriage. Be willing to give your all toward the marriage. She is yours, so there is no need to hold out. Don't think that you can exhaust the love that you pour out to her. Because the love of God has been poured into your heart by the Holy Spirit. Your source is a never-ending source of love. Your source is the Lord. When you give (not just money) it will be given back to you. Don't just receive the love of God; rather let His love flow through you. His love never fails; therefore, the source never fails. The only way your love toward your wife will fail is if you turn it off. If your love is on-again off-again, check the source. God not only told the husband to love his wife, He also provides the wisdom, ability, and the source. It's not your love; it's His love flowing through you.

Scriptural Foundation for "Husbands, Love your Wives..."

Ephesians 5:25-33

New International Version (NIV)

Husbands, love your wives, just as Christ loved the church and gave himself up for her to make her holy, cleansing her by the washing with water through the word, and to present her to himself as a radiant church, without stain or wrinkle or any other blemish, but holy and blameless. In this same way, husbands ought to love their wives as their own bodies. He who loves his wife loves himself. After all, no one ever hated his own body, but he feeds and cares for it, just as Christ does the church - for we are members of his body. "For this reason a man will leave his father and mother and be united to his wife, and the Two will become one flesh." This is a profound mystery - but I am talking about Christ and the church. However, each one of you also must love his wife as he loves himself, and the wife must respect her husband.

The Living Bible (TLB)

And you husbands, show the same kind of love to your wives as Christ showed to the Church when he died for her, to make her holy and clean, washed by baptism and God's Word; so that he could give her to himself as a glorious Church without a single spot or wrinkle or any other blemish, being holy and without a single fault. That is how husbands should treat their wives, loving them as parts of themselves. For since a man and his wife are now one, a man is really doing himself a favor and loving himself when he loves his wife! No one hates his own body but lovingly cares for it, just as Christ cares for his body the Church, of which we are parts. (That the husband and wife are one body is proved by the Scripture which says, "A man must leave his father and mother when he marries, so that he can be perfectly joined to his wife, and the two shall be one.") I know this is hard to understand, but it is an illustration of the way we are parts of the body of Christ. So again I say, a man must love his wife as a part of himself; and the wife must see to it that she deeply respects her husband – obeying, praising and honoring him.

The Amplified Bible (AMP)

Husbands, love your wives, as Christ loved the church and gave himself up for her, so that He might sanctify her, having cleansed her by the washing of water with the Word, that He might present the church to Himself in glorious splendor, without spot or wrinkle or any such things [that she might be holy and faultless]. Even so husbands should love their wives as [being in a sense] their own bodies. He who loves his own wife loves himself. For no man ever hated his own flesh, but nourishes *and* carefully protects and cherishes it, as Christ does the church. Because we are members (parts) of His body. For this reason a man shall leave his father and his mother and shall be joined to his wife, and the two shall become one flesh. This mystery is very great, but I speak concerning [the relation of] Christ and the church. However, let each man of you [without exception] love his wife as [being in a sense] his very own self; and let the wife see that she respects *and* reverences her husband [that she notices him, regards him, honors him, prefers him, venerates, and esteems him; and that she defers to him, praises him, and loves and admires him exceedingly].

The King James Version (KJV)

Husbands, love your wives, even as Christ also loved the church, and gave himself for it; that he might sanctify and cleanse it with the washing of water by the word, that he might present it to himself a glorious church, not having spot, or wrinkle, or any such thing; but that it should be holy and without blemish. So ought men to love their wives as their own bodies. He that loveth his wife loveth himself. For no man ever yet hated his own flesh; but nourisheth and cherisheth it, even as the Lord the church: For we are members of his body, of his flesh, and of his bones. For this cause shall a man leave his father and mother, and shall be joined unto his wife, and they two shall be one flesh. This is a great mystery: but I speak concerning Christ and the church. Nevertheless let every one of you in particular so love his wife even as himself; and the wife *see* that she reverence *her* husband.

Notes

HUSBANDS, LOVE YOUR WIVES...

A Collection of Devotions for Husbands and Wives

By Bobby & Pam Sanders

Email the Authors at: Loveyourwives@aol.com

For additional copies send $10.00 (check or money order $7.77 plus $2.23 shipping and handling) per book to:

Editor & Publisher
Bobby & Pam Sanders
Husbands, Love Your Wives Publications
P. O. Box 2142
Harker Heights, TX 76548-2142
(254) 699-3785

or contact your local bookstore to order
ISBN 1-59196-057-6